LLC BEGINNER'S GUIDE

ENTREPRENEUR'S GUIDEBOOK TO FORMING,
MANAGING, AND MAINTAINING YOUR SMALL
BUSINESS FOR SUCCESS WHILE BUILDING A STRONG
FOUNDATION AND BRAND

CONRAD PRESLEY

*Building a
Strong
Foundation*

The Entrepreneur's Guidebook to
Forming, Managing, and Maintaining
Your Small Business for Success
While Building a Strong Foundation

LLC
BEGINNER'S GUIDE

CONRAD PRESLEY

For permissions requests, speaking inquiries, and bulk order purchase options, email: publishing@uconcept.com.

ISBN: 978-1-960188-29-8 | E-book

ISBN: 978-1-960188-30-4 | Paperback

ISBN: 978-1-960188-31-1 | Hardcover

Published by Unlimited Concepts, Coconut Creek, Florida.

www.publishing.uconcept.com

Book, Editing, and Cover Design by Janet M Garcia | UConceptDesigns.com

To My Son...

I dedicate this book to my son, who has always been my biggest inspiration and motivation to pursue my dreams. His unwavering support and belief in me have pushed me to new heights, and I am forever grateful for his love and encouragement.

May this book serve as a reminder of the importance of following your passions and never giving up on your goals.

CONTENTS

INTRODUCTION

In recent years, there's been a notable surge in entrepreneurship, with more individuals than ever choosing to steer their futures by starting their own businesses. Among the various business structures available, Limited Liability Companies (LLCs) have become particularly popular due to their flexibility and the protection they offer to business owners. However, the process of forming and managing an LLC involves navigating a maze of legal and financial considerations that can be daunting for both new and experienced entrepreneurs alike. This book will demystify these complexities, providing you with a clear, easy-to-follow guide on how to effectively set up and run your LLC.

My passion for assisting entrepreneurs like you is rooted in years of experience in business consultancy, where I've specialized in advising on the formation, management, and expansion of LLCs. The insights shared in this book are drawn from real-world scenarios, refined through the lens of my professional journey, aimed at delivering practical, actionable advice. My goal is to equip you with the knowledge and tools necessary to navigate the challenges of business ownership, enabling you to focus on what truly matters - growing your business.

What sets this book apart is its holistic approach, blending legal, financial, and managerial advice into a singular, accessible resource. Whether you're contemplating launching your first business or you're an established entrepreneur looking to structure your business operations under an LLC, this guide is designed for you. It breaks down complex concepts into simple, understandable language, complemented by real-world examples and case studies that bring these concepts to life.

As you turn these pages, I encourage you to approach this book not just as a collection of information, but as a companion in your entrepreneurial journey. Engage with the content, apply the lessons learned, and step forward with confidence, knowing you are well-equipped to succeed in the dynamic world of business.

Welcome to your guide to mastering the LLC with confidence and clarity. Let's get started on building a strong foundation for your business success.

THE BASICS OF LLCS

*D*id you know that over the last decade, the number of new LLCs registered each year has nearly doubled? This spike isn't just a trend; it's a clear indicator of the shift in the business landscape where more individuals are seizing control of their economic futures. The choice of business structure is paramount, not only in defining the trajectory of your business but in safeguarding your personal assets and managing your tax obligations efficiently. In this opening chapter, we'll explore the foundational elements of Limited Liability Companies (LLCs), a structure that combines the ease of a partnership with the solid protections of a corporation, making it a preferred choice for many entrepreneurs and small business owners.

WHAT IS AN LLC AND WHY CHOOSE THIS STRUCTURE?

Definition and Origins

A Limited Liability Company (LLC) is a versatile business entity legally distinct from its owners, who are known as members. Originating from the German GmbH law in the late 19th century and later adopted by the US state of Wyoming in 1977, the LLC was designed to provide business owners with the liability protection usually reserved for corporations, without the accompanying rigorous tax and administrative burdens. Today, LLCs are recognized across all 50 states and are lauded for their adaptability to different business operations, combining the operational simplicity and tax benefits of partnerships with the corporate advantage of limited liability.

Benefits of Choosing an LLC

One of the most significant advantages of forming an LLC is personal asset protection. As an LLC member, your personal assets—like your home, car, and savings—are protected from business debts and claims. In essence, should your business face a lawsuit or fail to meet its financial obligations, your personal assets would generally remain secure. Beyond this, LLCs are known for their tax flexibility. Unlike corporations, which are subject to double taxation, LLCs benefits pass-through taxation. This means that business profits are passed directly to members and reported on their personal tax returns, thus avoiding the corporate tax level. Additionally, LLCs offer operational ease, with fewer record-keeping requirements and more flexibility in management and profit distribution.

Despite their advantages, several myths surround LLCs. Some believe that LLCs are overly complicated or only advantageous for large businesses. However, LLCs can be an ideal choice even for solo entrepreneurs who want liability protection with minimal administrative overhead. Another common misconception is that forming an LLC is prohibitively expensive. In reality, the cost of setting up and maintaining an LLC is relatively modest and can offer significant financial benefits and protections that far outweigh these initial and ongoing expenses.

Real-World Applications

Consider the story of a freelance graphic designer who transitioned from a sole proprietor to forming an LLC. Despite initial reservations about the process and costs, the designer soon found that having an LLC not only provided a safety net against potential liabilities but also elevated the business's credibility, attracting more substantial clients. Moreover, the LLC structure allowed more straightforward and beneficial tax arrangements, significantly reducing the yearly tax burdens. Another example is a small organic bakery that started as a family partnership. Transitioning to an LLC helped the owners protect their personal assets from the business's debts and facilitated easier access to capital for expansion, through more formalized financial statements that were attractive to potential investors.

These practical applications underscore how LLCs can serve varied business needs, providing flexibility, protection, and growth potential. As we delve deeper into the operational aspects of LLCs in the following sections, keep these examples in mind as a testament to the practical benefits and robust protection offered by this business structure. Remember, the right foundation is not just about starting your business—it's about setting the stage for sustainable success and growth.

LLCS COMPARED: PROS AND CONS AGAINST OTHER BUSINESS STRUCTURES

When considering the structure of your business, understanding the differences between an LLC and other forms of business entities such as sole proprietorships, partnerships, and corporations is crucial. Each has its unique advantages and limitations, primarily revolving around issues of liability, taxation, and operational flexibility. This section aims to provide you with a clear perspective on why an LLC might be the preferable choice for your business, depending on your specific needs, goals, and risk tolerance.

Comparison with Sole Proprietorships and Partnerships

Sole proprietorships and general partnerships are among the simplest and most common forms of business entities due to their ease of formation and minimal regulatory requirements. However, they offer no personal liability protection, meaning personal assets like your home, car, or savings could be at risk if your business incurs debt or is sued. This is where LLCs present a significant advantage. An LLC legally separates your personal assets from those of your business, providing a shield against personal liability. This means that only the assets within the business can be targeted by lawsuits or creditors. Additionally, while sole proprietorships and partnerships report business income on personal tax returns, which might seem advantageous, they lack the opportunities for tax planning that an LLC offers. Even though LLCs benefit from pass-through taxation, you can also choose to have it taxed as a corporation, providing flexibility to optimize tax liabilities based on the evolving circumstances of your business.

Differences from Corporations

Corporations are structured to offer strong liability protection but at the cost of significant administrative overhead and rigid operational structures. They are often subject to double taxation—once at the corporate level and again on dividends paid to shareholders. In contrast, LLCs offer similar liability protections without the burden of double taxation, thanks to their pass-through tax status. Moreover, LLCs provide operational flexibility absent in corporate structures. For instance, corporations require a formal management structure consisting of a board of directors and officers. LLCs, however, allow owners to directly manage the business or appoint managers. This flexibility is particularly beneficial for small to medium-sized business owners who prefer direct control over day-to-day operations without the formalities and compliance issues that corporations face.

Deciding on the right business structure requires a careful assessment of your business's current needs and future goals. Consider factors such as the level of liability protection needed, the tax implications, the ability to attract investment, and the administrative overhead you are prepared to handle. For many small businesses and entrepreneurs, an LLC offers the right balance of protection, flexibility, and efficiency. However, if you are planning to seek significant outside investment or eventually go public, the corporate structure might be more suitable despite its complexities. It's essential to weigh these factors in light of your specific business goals and consult with a legal or financial advisor to make the most informed decision.

• Case Studies

Several real-world examples highlight the impact of transitioning to an LLC from other business structures. Take, for instance, a boutique marketing firm initially started as a partnership. The partners decided to convert the business into an LLC as it grew and the potential for liability increased. This transition not only protected the partners' personal assets but also improved their ability to secure business loans and contracts, as the LLC structure was viewed as more credible and stable by financial institutions and clients. Another case involved a tech startup initially incorporated as a corporation due to its plans to attract venture capital. As the business landscape and goals shifted, the company transitioned to an LLC to benefit from tax advantages and reduce the administrative burden, significantly cutting down on costs and increasing operational flexibility. These cases exemplify how the choice of business structure can fundamentally impact your company's financial health, liability, and overall success.

UNDERSTANDING LLC LEGAL PROTECTIONS FOR PERSONAL ASSETS

One of the most compelling reasons entrepreneurs opt for an LLC is the level of protection it offers for personal assets. This protection is rooted in the legal principle known as "limited liability," which is fundamental to the LLC's appeal. Limited liability means that as an owner, or 'member,' of an LLC, you are not personally liable for the company's debts or legal liabilities. Essentially, your personal assets—such as your home, personal bank accounts, and personal belongings—are shielded from creditors and legal judgments against your business. This separation acts as a fortress safeguarding your personal estate from any business misfortunes, which can be a frequent risk in entrepreneurship.

However, it's crucial to recognize that this shield is not impenetrable. There are scenarios where personal liability can still arise.

For instance, if you personally guarantee a business loan or a commercial lease, you explicitly agree to be personally liable for that obligation. This means that should the LLC fail to meet these liabilities, creditors can legally pursue your personal assets. Another common situation is if you engage in fraudulent business practices. Courts can 'pierce the corporate veil,' a legal term used to describe the action of treating the rights or duties of a corporation as the rights or liabilities of its shareholders or members. In such cases, if a court determines that the LLC was merely an alter-ego or a facade for personal dealings, or if you commingled personal and business funds, it might hold you personally liable for business debts.

To reinforce the protection your LLC provides, it is advisable to adhere strictly to corporate formalities. This includes maintaining a clear separation of personal and business finances. It is wise to have separate bank accounts and credit cards for your business, and always conduct transactions under the business name rather than your personal name. Additionally, ensuring that all business agreements, contracts, and leases are made in the name of the LLC and not your name is crucial. These steps not only strengthen the liability shield but also enhance the credibility and integrity of your business in the eyes of the law, creditors, and business partners.

Let's look at real-life scenarios where the protection of personal assets within an LLC was upheld in court. In one notable case, the owner of a small construction firm faced a lawsuit due to an injury that occurred on the job site. Because the business was structured as an LLC and the owner had diligently kept personal and business finances separate, the court ruled that the owner's personal assets were not subject to claims for damages. This ruling not only protected the owner's personal estate but also underscored the importance of proper LLC management. Another scenario involved a multi-member LLC that faced bankruptcy. The court scrutinized the company's records and operations and found that all members had adhered to the legal requirements and formalities of operating an LLC. Consequently, the members' personal assets were protected from creditors, highlighting how critical adherence to legal formalities is for asset protection.

These examples emphasize the effectiveness of LLCs in protecting personal assets when members respect the structure's operational boundaries and legal requirements. While the protection is robust, it requires diligence and proper management to ensure that the benefits of an LLC can be fully realized and legally upheld. As you continue to build and grow your business, keeping these principles in mind will not only safeguard your personal assets but also fortify the foundation upon which your business operates.

THE FLEXIBILITY OF LLCS: MANAGEMENT AND OWNERSHIP STRUCTURES

One of the most compelling attributes of an LLC is its inherent flexibility in management and ownership structures, which can be tailored to meet the specific needs and goals of its members. This adaptability is crucial, especially in a business environment where operational dynamics can change rapidly. Understanding how these structures function and how you can best utilize them is vital for leveraging the full potential of your LLC.

Management Options

LLCs offer two primary management structures: member-managed and manager-managed. In a member-managed LLC, all members (owners) actively participate in the business's daily management decisions. This structure is akin to a partnership, where each member has a say in the operational decisions, and it works well for smaller LLCs or those where all members wish to be equally involved in managing the business. Conversely, a manager-managed LLC involves appointing one or more managers who may (or may not) be members themselves. These managers handle the LLC's daily operations, while the members are not as involved in the day-to-day affairs but focus on broader, strategic decisions. This setup is ideal for larger LLCs or those where members prefer to be passive investors rather than active managers.

Choosing between these management structures depends largely on the number of members, their individual expertise, and their interest in daily business operations. For instance, if your LLC has members who prefer to invest rather than participate in day-to-day management, a manager-managed structure might be more appropriate. This decision also affects how decisions are made within the LLC, impacting everything from financial management to strategic planning. It's crucial to outline this structure in the LLC's operating agreement, ensuring clarity and preventing conflicts among members.

Ownership Flexibility

LLCs are remarkably flexible when it comes to ownership. They can be owned by one person (a single-member LLC) or have many owners (multi-member LLC), and there are no upper limits on the number of members. Additionally, LLCs offer flexibility in how ownership percentages are structured. Unlike corporations, where ownership is determined by the number of shares held, LLC ownership can be allocated through varying percentages that do not necessarily correlate with the members' investment amounts. For example, two members might contribute different amounts of capital but still opt for equal ownership percentages based on their roles or expected contributions to the business.

This flexibility in defining ownership and distributing profits allows LLCs to tailor their financial and operational strategies to fit their unique business model and the specific needs of their members. However, it is essential to clearly document these arrangements in the operating agreement to avoid any misunderstandings or disputes among members down the line.

Decision-Making in LLCs

Decision-making in an LLC is governed by the rules set out in the operating agreement, which acts as a framework for both daily management and broader strategic decisions. This agreement should specify who gets to make which decisions and the processes through which decisions must be made. In a member-managed LLC, all members typically have equal rights in decision-making, unless the operating agreement specifies otherwise. In manager-managed LLCs, managers handle most operational decisions, but significant decisions like amending the operating agreement or selling the business may require a vote among the members.

The operating agreement can also specify the voting rights of each member, which might be proportional to ownership interests or equal regardless of ownership percentage. This clarity in decision-making processes and rights is crucial for the smooth operation of the business and helps in preventing conflicts among members or between members and managers.

Examples of Successful Management Structures

The versatility of LLCs in tailoring management and ownership to fit specific needs can be seen in numerous real-world applications. For instance, a web design startup initially structured as a member-managed LLC allowed its founders to be directly involved in all aspects of the business during its early stages. As the startup grew, it transitioned to a manager-managed structure to accommodate the less hands-on approach of new investors and to delegate daily operations to a skilled management team, allowing the founders to focus on strategic growth.

Another example is a family-owned restaurant that operated successfully under a member-managed structure, where all family members shared management responsibilities. Their operating agreement clearly defined the role and decision-making power of each member, which was crucial in maintaining harmony and clarity in business operations. These examples demonstrate that whether opting for a hands-on approach in a member-managed model or delegating day-to-day tasks in a manager-managed framework, LLCs offer the flexibility to adapt the management structure as the business evolves. This adaptability not only facilitates operational efficiency but also supports sustainable growth, making LLCs a preferred choice for many entrepreneurs and investors.

STATE-SPECIFIC LLC FORMATION REQUIREMENTS: A COMPREHENSIVE OVERVIEW

There are state-specific regulations that can significantly influence your decision on where and how to establish your LLC. Every state in the U.S. offers its unique blend of fees, legal requirements, and ongoing obligations that can affect both the immediate costs of setting up your LLC and its long-term operational ease. Understanding these variations is crucial as they can impact everything from your business's legal protection to its tax liabilities and administrative burdens.

Variability of State Regulations

Each state has its individual rules regarding the formation, operation, and dissolution of LLCs. These rules encompass everything from the initial setup fees, which can vary dramatically from one state to another, to the annual or biennial fees required to maintain good standing. Additionally, states differ in their requirements for maintaining internal records and making these records available for public inspection. For example, some states require LLCs to file annual reports detailing updates on business activities and changes in membership or management, which usually come with a filing fee. On the other hand, a few states impose no such annual reporting requirements, potentially reducing administrative tasks for LLCs incorporated there.

Furthermore, the tax regulations affecting LLCs can also differ significantly by state. While LLCs typically benefit from pass-through taxation at the federal level, some states impose an additional franchise tax or capital values tax on LLCs. Understanding these nuances is vital in planning your business strategy and financial management practices. For instance, if your business is in a sector with high revenue but low profit margins, operating in a state with no franchise tax on LLCs might save substantial amounts of money annually.

Choosing a State for Your LLC

The decision on where to establish your LLC should not be taken lightly. While many entrepreneurs opt to register their LLCs in their home state to simplify operations, others might consider different states based on strategic advantages. Factors to consider include the state's legal environment, taxation policies, and the overall business climate. States like Delaware, Wyoming, and Nevada are popular choices for LLC formation due to their business-friendly laws, including enhanced privacy protections, minimal reporting requirements, and favorable tax laws. For instance, Nevada offers the advantage of no state corporate income tax and no fees on corporate shares, while Delaware is known for its well-established law regarding LLCs and business entities, providing a clear legal framework and strong protections for company owners.

However, forming an LLC outside of your home state is not without complications. It often means qualifying as a "foreign LLC" in your home state and complying with the regulations and fees in both states. This can lead to increased paperwork and costs, potentially offsetting the benefits gained from the favorable laws of the state in which the LLC was formed. Therefore, a detailed analysis comparing the long-term benefits and drawbacks is essential before making this decision.

Most states have dedicated websites that provide comprehensive information on the steps required to form an LLC, including downloadable forms and fee schedules. These resources are invaluable for ensuring compliance with state-specific legal requirements and for staying updated on any changes to business laws. For example, the California Secretary of State's website offers a portal where entrepreneurs can file for LLC formation online, access detailed guides on state requirements, and even sign up for alerts on updates to business laws.

Leveraging these online resources not only helps in forming your LLC but also in maintaining its good standing through timely compliance with annual filings and fee payments. Many states provide online systems where annual reports and fees can be submitted electronically, simplifying what could otherwise be a cumbersome administrative task.

In Texas, LLCs are subject to a relatively high formation fee but benefit from no state income tax, which can be particularly advantageous for high-earning businesses. In contrast, while Massachusetts charges lower initial filing fees, it imposes an annual LLC fee that is one of the highest in the country. This recurring fee can add up, making it a less attractive option for businesses with tighter budgets.

Another example is the comparison between New York and Arizona. New York requires LLCs to comply with a publication requirement, where the formation of the LLC must be published in a local newspaper, which can add over a thousand dollars to the initial cost of forming an LLC. Arizona, on the other hand, has no such requirement, which may make it a more cost-effective option, especially for businesses that are mindful of upfront expenses.

These examples underscore the importance of a thorough understanding of state-specific requirements when forming an LLC. By carefully weighing these factors, you can choose a state that not only meets your business needs but also enhances your opportunities for financial efficiency and legal protection.

THE LIFECYCLE OF AN LLC: FROM FORMATION TO DISSOLUTION

Understanding the lifecycle of an LLC from its inception to its cessation is crucial for maintaining legal compliance and maximizing the benefits of the LLC structure. This lifecycle encompasses various stages, each requiring specific actions and considerations to ensure the smooth operation and eventual orderly dissolution of the LLC if necessary. Here, we will explore these stages in detail, providing a roadmap for the formation, ongoing compliance, and dissolution processes, complemented by real-life case studies to illustrate these concepts in action.

Formation Steps

The formation of an LLC is the first step in its lifecycle and involves several key actions. Initially, you must file the Articles of Organization with the state agency responsible for business filings, like the Secretary of State's office, for example. This document serves as the official birth certificate of your LLC, outlining basic information such as the LLC's name, principal address, and the names of its members. The filing of this document usually incurs a fee, which varies by state.

Following the filing, creating an Operating Agreement is imperative, though not always legally required. This internal document outlines the ownership structure, member responsibilities, and operational procedures of the LLC. It acts as a cornerstone for managing the LLC's operations and resolving any disputes that may arise among members. The Operating Agreement should be comprehensive and tailored to fit the specific needs and goals of the business and its members, detailing everything from the distribution of profits and losses to the protocols for adding new members or handling the departure of existing ones.

The final step in the formation process is obtaining any necessary business licenses and permits, which vary depending on the LLC's location and industry. Additionally, an Employer Identification Number (EIN) must be obtained from the Internal Revenue

Service (IRS) to open a bank account, hire employees, and comply with tax requirements. This number is essentially the social security number for your business and is crucial for maintaining corporate separation between the LLC and its members.

Once established, maintaining an LLC requires adherence to a series of regulatory and fiscal responsibilities to ensure its good standing with state and federal agencies. This includes the annual or biennial filing of reports and the associated fees with the state of formation. These filings provide updates on the LLC's address, management structure, and other pertinent details that may have changed over the year. Failure to comply with these requirements can lead to penalties or even administrative dissolution of the LLC.

Tax compliance is also a significant aspect of an LLC's lifecycle. Specific tax forms must be filed, and appropriate taxes paid, such as self-employment taxes and payroll taxes if the LLC has employees. Regular consultations with a tax advisor are advisable to navigate the complex tax landscape effectively and take advantage of potential tax benefits.

Dissolving an LLC

The dissolution of an LLC is as critical a process as its formation and requires careful attention to legal and fiscal responsibilities to ensure a clean closure of the business. The process begins with a formal decision to dissolve, typically requiring a vote according to the stipulations in the Operating Agreement. Following this decision, the Articles of Dissolution must be filed with the state to officially end the LLC's existence.

A crucial part of dissolution is settling debts and obligations. The LLC must notify creditors of its dissolution and settle all outstanding debts. Any remaining assets after settling debts are then distributed among the members according to their ownership percentages as stipulated in the Operating Agreement. It is also necessary to cancel any business licenses and permits and close out business tax accounts with the IRS and state tax agencies.

BOI E-FILING SYSTEM FOR LLC

BOI are the Beneficial Ownership Information Reports of your LLC. The BOI E-Filing system for Limited Liability Companies (LLC) serves as a digital platform designed to facilitate the efficient and streamlined submission of various business-related documents and forms by LLC entities. This electronic system leverages technology to enable seamless online interactions between LLCs and the Board of Investment (BOI), thereby enhancing the overall operational effectiveness and regulatory compliance within the business landscape. Through the utilization of this advanced e-filing mechanism, LLCs can conveniently submit, process, and track a wide array of essential documentation with enhanced precision and expediency.

Furthermore, the implementation of the BOI E-Filing system for LLC embodies a paradigm shift in contemporary administrative practices by fostering a digitized environment that encourages greater transparency, accountability, and accessibility in regulatory processes. By harnessing the power of digital platforms, this pioneering initiative underscores a progressive approach towards modernizing traditional bureaucratic procedures while promoting a more agile and responsive regulatory framework within the context of LLC operations. As such, the BOI E-Filing system for LLC facilitates smoother regulatory compliance mechanisms for businesses operating within dynamic economic ecosystems.

Companies registered before January 1, 2024 will have one year to file. On the other hand, companies registered on or after January 1, 2024 will have to file within 90 days. If the LLC will be formed on or after January 1, 2025, you will have only 30 days to file from registration date.

Failing to Report Accurately and Truthfully

If you fail to fail to report the beneficial ownership information with *accuracy* and *truthfully*, you may face a daily civil penalty up to $500 for every day the violation continues, and you may also face a criminal penalty of $10,000 and/or up to 2 years of imprisonment.

You can now see how crucial is filing your BOI for the operation of your LLC business once it's registered.

FORMING YOUR LLC

The initial stages of forming an LLC entail navigating a series of crucial paperwork, which, while seemingly mundane, are foundational to your business's legal identity and operational success. This chapter aims to guide you through these initial steps, focusing on the pivotal task of preparing and filing the Articles of Organization.

NAVIGATING THE PAPERWORK: ARTICLES OF ORGANIZATION EXPLAINED

Understanding Articles of Organization

The Articles of Organization, sometimes known as the *Certificate of Formation* or *Articles of Incorporation* depending on your state, is the primary document required to legally establish an LLC in the United States. This document needs to be filed with the state agency that handles business filings, typically the Secretary of State's office. The Articles of Organization serve several vital functions; they officially register the existence of your LLC under state law, establish the basic structure of your business, and protect your personal assets by legally separating them from those of the business.

The key components of the Articles of Organization generally include the name of the LLC, its principal office address, the duration of the LLC (if not perpetual), the purpose of the business (often stated in broad terms to allow flexibility), and information about the registered agent and the LLC's management structure (whether it is member-managed or manager-managed). Each of these elements plays a crucial role in defining how your business operates and how it is perceived legally and commercially.

Filing Process and Requirements

Filing the Articles of Organization involves a step-by-step process. First, you must ensure that the LLC's name is available and adheres to your state's naming guidelines, including avoiding confusion with existing business names and including an LLC designator, such as "Limited Liability Company" or its abbreviations (LLC, L.L.C.).

Once the name is secured, you can proceed to fill out the Articles of Organization form, which can typically be downloaded from the state's business filing agency's website. This form must be completed with accuracy, detailing all required information such as the LLC's official name, principal office address, and the registered agent's name and address. The registered agent is responsible for receiving legal documents on behalf of the LLC and must be available during regular business hours.

After completing the form, it must be submitted along with the filing fee, which varies by state. Some states allow for online filing, which can expedite the process, while others might require a mailed physical copy. It is crucial during this stage to double-check all entered information for accuracy and completeness to avoid delays or rejections of your filing.

It's important to recognize that specific requirements for the Articles of Organization can vary significantly by state. Some states may require additional information, such as details about the LLC's members and managers, or may have different requirements regarding the registered agent's qualifications. Moreover, the cost of filing the Articles of Organization can range from as little as $50 to over $300, depending on the state.

For example, some states like New York require newly formed LLCs to publish a notice in a local newspaper about the LLC formation, which can add to the cost and the procedural steps you need to undertake. Other states might have minimal requirements but higher annual fees or taxes that need to be considered as part of your broader financial planning.

In this chapter, we have unpacked the crucial initial steps of forming your LLC, with a particular focus on understanding and filing the Articles of Organization. This document is not merely a formality but a foundational step in legally establishing your business and protecting your personal assets. As you move forward, remember that each decision and detail, no matter how small, contributes to the strength and stability of your LLC. With careful attention to the guidelines provided and mindful consideration of the specifics of your state's requirements, you are well on your way to turning your business idea into a legal and operational reality.

CHOOSING YOUR LLC'S NAME: LEGAL REQUIREMENTS AND BRANDING STRATEGIES

Selecting the right name for your LLC is a crucial decision that impacts your brand's identity and legal standing. When you choose a name for your LLC, you are not merely picking a label under which your business will operate, but you are also making a strategic decision that will influence your marketing efforts and public perception. Let's discuss how to navigate the process of naming your LLC, ensuring it not only meets state legal requirements but also positions your brand effectively in the marketplace.

Name Availability and Restrictions

The first step in naming your LLC involves checking the availability of your desired name to ensure it is not already in use by another business in your state. This is typically done through a name search on your state's Secretary of State website, where you can enter your proposed name and see if there are any existing businesses registered under the same or a highly similar name. It's crucial to perform this search diligently because using a name that's already taken can lead to legal disputes and confusion in the market.

State naming requirements also dictate that your LLC's name must include an identifier such as "LLC," "L.L.C.," or "Limited Liability Company" to clearly indicate that it is a legal entity separate from its owners. Some states may have additional restrictions, such as prohibiting certain words that could mislead the public about the nature of the business (e.g., "bank," "insurance," "federal"). Ensuring compliance with these rules not only avoids the rejection of your filing but also clarifies your business's structure to consumers and other businesses.

Branding Implications & Trademark Considerations

The name of your LLC plays a pivotal role in your branding and marketing initiatives. A strong, memorable name creates a lasting impression on consumers and can significantly influence the perceived value and professionalism of your business. It should convey something meaningful about your business, whether it's the services you offer, the core values of your brand, or the unique selling proposition that sets you apart from competitors. For instance, a tech company might choose a name that reflects innovation and speed, while a sustainable clothing brand might opt for a name that evokes nature and renewal.

Your business name is often the first point of contact between your company and potential customers, making it a vital tool in building brand identity. It should resonate with your target audience, be easy to pronounce and remember, and have the potential for visual representation in a logo. This name will appear on your marketing materials, business cards, website, and social media platforms, so choosing a name that aligns with your branding strategy is essential for creating a cohesive and strong market presence.

While checking for name availability with your state is necessary, it's also wise to consider federal trademark implications. Conducting a trademark search through the United States Patent and Trademark Office (USPTO) can tell you whether your chosen name or similar names are trademarked nationally. Using a name that is already trademarked can lead to legal challenges and force you to rebrand, a costly and damaging process for any business, especially after initial marketing efforts and brand establishment.

If your chosen name is available, you might consider registering it as a trademark to protect your brand at a national level, granting you exclusive rights to the name across all states. This is particularly important if you plan to do business outside your state or expand in the future. Securing a trademark can safeguard your brand identity and prevent others from using a name that could be confused with yours in critical markets.

To select a name, start with brainstorming sessions focusing on your business's core values, target audience, and industry specifics. Tools like online name generators can spark ideas, but the most compelling names often come from deep thinking about what makes your business unique.

Consider involving your team in the naming process for a broader perspective, or even crowdsource ideas from potential customers through social media to gauge public reaction and get people invested in your brand from the start. Remember, a good business name not only meets legal requirements and strengthens your branding but also connects emotionally with your audience, setting the stage for your business's story and marketing narrative.

ASSIGNING A REGISTERED AGENT FOR YOUR LLC

When you establish an LLC, one of the key roles you need to fill is that of the registered agent. This role is not just a formality but a critical component in ensuring that your business meets legal requirements and operates smoothly. A registered agent acts as the official point of contact for receiving all governmental correspondence, including service of process notices, legal summons, and important documents from the state. This role is pivotal because it ensures that any legal actions taken against your LLC are addressed promptly and properly, preventing default judgments against your business.

The primary responsibility of a registered agent is to be available to receive legal documents on behalf of the LLC. This includes accepting lawsuits and other legal documents and then forwarding these documents to the appropriate individual within your LLC. Beyond handling legal paperwork, registered agents may also receive important tax forms, renewal reminders from the state, and other official communications. Essentially, the registered agent serves as the critical communication link between your LLC and the state government, ensuring that you stay informed of and respond to legal and tax-related documents in a timely manner.

Requirements for Registered Agents

There are specific legal requirements that a registered agent must meet, which vary slightly by state. However, universally, a registered agent must have a physical address (not a P.O. Box) in the state where your LLC is registered. This requirement is crucial because it ensures that someone is always available to receive documents in person. Another key requirement is that the registered agent must be available at this address during normal business hours to facilitate the delivery of legal documents and to comply with state laws that aim to prevent businesses from avoiding legal actions or responsibilities. It's important to note that while you can serve as your own registered agent, doing so can present privacy and practicality issues, especially if you do not maintain regular business hours at a consistent location.

Choosing a Registered Agent

Selecting the right registered agent is a decision that should be approached with care. You have two primary options: appointing an individual, such as yourself or another member of the LLC, or hiring a professional registered agent service. While appointing an individual might seem like a cost-effective choice, there are significant advantages to using a professional service. Professional registered agents ensure that there is always someone available if you don't have a fixed office location or if you travel frequently. Additionally, using a professional service provides an added layer of privacy, as the registered agent's address will be listed on public records, rather than your personal or business address.

When choosing a registered agent service, consider factors such as reliability, privacy, experience, and the additional services they may offer, such as compliance alerts or document storage. It's also wise to review their standing with the Better Business Bureau and look for customer feedback to gauge their reputation and reliability. Remember, the peace of mind that comes from knowing your legal documents are being handled promptly and professionally can often outweigh the cost of a registered agent service.

If at any point you decide to change your registered agent, whether it's switching to a different service or appointing a new individual, the process generally involves filing a change of agent form with your state's business filing agency. This form updates the state with the new agent's name and address. There is typically a nominal fee associated with filing this change. It's crucial to ensure that there is no lapse in coverage when switching agents. Before dismissing your current agent, have the new one ready to step in and ensure that all parties are informed about the change to prevent any miscommunication or mishandling of legal documents.

Selecting and maintaining a registered agent is a fundamental aspect of your LLC's compliance with state laws. This role, while often underestimated, can significantly impact your business's legal integrity and operational smoothness. By choosing wisely and ensuring your registered agent meets all legal requirements, you safeguard your business's standing and ensure it continues to operate uninterrupted within the legal frameworks established by your state.

DRAFTING YOUR LLC OPERATING AGREEMENT: A BLUEPRINT FOR SUCCESS

The Operating Agreement of an LLC functions as the architectural blueprint for your business, laying out the guidelines under which your business will operate and preemptively resolving potential conflicts by clarifying the rules and expectations for all members. This document, while not universally required by law, is fundamentally important—even for single-member LLCs—because it establishes your company's operational procedures and solidifies your limited liability protection by showing that your LLC is operating as a separate business entity.

Importance & Key Components of an Operating Agreement

An Operating Agreement enhances the credibility of your LLC by providing a clear framework that can be referred to in legal situations to demonstrate that your LLC is a separate entity from yourself. This separation is essential for protecting personal assets in legal disputes. For multi-member LLCs, this agreement sets forth how decisions are made, profits are shared, and disputes are resolved, which can prevent costly and time-consuming disagreements. In the case of single-member LLCs, the Operating Agreement proves to banks and potential investors that a formal structure is in place, which can be pivotal in financial and legal transactions.

A robust Operating Agreement should include several key sections to comprehensively cover the governance of your LLC. Firstly, it should outline the ownership structure, detailing each member's percentage interest in the LLC, which directly influences voting power and profit shares. This section should clearly align owner-ship percentages with capital contributions or specify any special arrangements that deviate from this norm.

Another critical component is the distribution of profits and losses. Specifying how and when profits will be distributed, and losses allocated is essential for financial planning and can help avert financial disputes among members. Additionally, the agreement should dictate the management structure of the LLC, distinguishing between member-managed and manager-managed, and detailing the specific powers and duties assigned to managers or managing members.

The agreement should also include clauses on how decisions are made, specifying what types of decisions require a vote, and what percentage of votes is needed for different kinds of decisions. This can range from everyday operational decisions to major ones like amending the Operating Agreement or dissolving the LLC.

Finally, it should cover the induction of new members and the exit of existing members, detailing how membership interests can be transferred and the steps necessary to bring new members into the LLC. This part of the agreement ensures that there's a clear path for the evolution of your LLC's membership without causing disruption or disputes.

Tailoring your Operating Agreement to reflect the unique aspects of your LLC is vital in safeguarding your business's operations and your interests. For instance, if your LLC operates in an industry where sudden changes in membership could affect the business's stability or regulatory compliance, you might include more stringent rules for transferring membership interests. Alternatively, if your LLC is family-owned, you might incorporate special provisions for the succession of family members into the business.

Moreover, customizing your agreement allows you to incorporate any agreed-upon verbal understandings into the formal structure of your LLC, making these understandings enforceable and reducing the risk of misunderstandings or assumptions that could lead to disputes.

Common Pitfalls to Avoid

When drafting your Operating Agreement, several common oversights could lead to conflicts or legal challenges down the road. One major pitfall is vagueness; every clause should be as clear and specific as possible to avoid different interpretations that could lead to internal conflicts. For example, rather than simply stating that profits are to be distributed "fairly," specify the exact formula for how profits will be divided among members.

Another oversight is failing to plan for the future. Your Operating Agreement should include provisions for a variety of potential future scenarios, such as the bankruptcy of a member, the dissolution of the LLC, or the amendment of the Operating Agreement itself. Including such provisions ensures that your LLC is prepared for whatever may come, and isn't caught off-guard by unforeseen events.

Lastly, neglecting to have the Operating Agreement reviewed by a legal professional can be a critical mistake. Even if the agreement has been drafted with the utmost care, having it reviewed by a legal expert can help identify potential issues and ensure that the agreement complies with state laws and effectively protects the members' interests.

Drafting a thorough and customized Operating Agreement is an investment in your LLC's success and stability. By paying careful attention to the details and anticipating potential changes and challenges, you can create a strong foundation that supports your business's growth and safeguards its—and your—interests.

OBTAINING LICENSES AND PERMITS: STAYING COMPLIANT

Staying compliant with various regulatory requirements is not just a legal necessity but a cornerstone of building a trustworthy and sustainable business. For your LLC, this means obtaining the necessary licenses and permits at the local, state, and federal levels. These credentials are as vital as they are varied, depending on the nature of your business activities, the industry you are operating within, and the locations where your business has a footprint.

When initiating the process of gathering your business licenses and permits, a meticulous approach to research is crucial. Start by identifying the specific requirements that pertain to your business. This task can be daunting, given the wide range of industries and the different regulations that apply to each. Generally, most businesses will require some form of a basic operation license, which allows you to legally operate your business in your city or county. However, depending on your business type, additional specialized permits or licenses might be necessary. For instance, a restaurant might need health permits, liquor licenses, and signage permits, among others.

The best starting point is usually your local city or county government's website, where you can find information pertaining to required licenses and permits. For state and federal licenses, the U.S. Small Business Administration (SBA) offers a wealth of resources that can guide you through the types of licenses you need and direct you to the appropriate agencies. Remember, each type of license or permit has its own application process and fees, and it's vital to understand these details upfront to budget both time and money accordingly.

Operating across multiple locations introduces another layer of complexity to compliance. If your LLC operates in more than one city, county, or state, you must comply with the licensing requirements in each jurisdiction. This might mean multiple business licenses or various types of permits, each with their own renewal schedules and compliance stipulations. Keeping track of these can become challenging. It's beneficial to maintain a centralized database or use a compliance management system where all your licenses and permits, along with their expiry dates and renewal requirements, are systematically recorded. This system not only helps in staying organized but also ensures that no critical compliance deadlines are missed, which could lead to fines or disruptions in business operations.

Most licenses and permits have expiration dates and specific renewal procedures that must be strictly followed to avoid lapses in legal operations. Setting up reminders for renewal deadlines and understanding the renewal process are essential practices. Some jurisdictions might require a new set of documents or inspections before renewal approval, so being prepared well in advance of the renewal date is advisable. For instance, health permits for restaurants are often contingent on passing health inspections that assess compliance with safety and sanitation standards. Being prepared for these inspections ensures that the renewal process goes smoothly and that your business does not face any operational hiccups.

By thoroughly understanding and meticulously managing these requirements, you can ensure that your business operations flow smoothly and remain uninterrupted by compliance issues. This proactive stance not only safeguards your business against legal challenges but also builds its reputation as a reliable and responsible entity in the marketplace.

THE EIN: YOUR LLC'S TAX ID AND WHY IT MATTERS

Navigating the financial aspects of your LLC involves understanding and managing various identifiers and numbers, chief among them being the *Employer Identification Number (EIN)*. Known also as the *Federal Tax Identification Number*, the EIN is essentially the 'social security number' for your business. It's a unique nine-digit number that the Internal Revenue Service (IRS) assigns to identify your business for tax purposes and is crucial for a multitude of business activities.

Every LLC that engages in certain business activities, including hiring employees, operating as a corporation, or filing Employment, Excise, or Alcohol/Tobacco/Firearms tax returns, needs an EIN. Furthermore, most banks require an EIN to open a business bank account. The IRS also uses this number to track your business's tax obligations and filings, making it indispensable for maintaining your LLC's tax compliance. Even if your LLC does not hire employees, obtaining an EIN can still be beneficial. It helps protect your personal information by allowing you to use your EIN instead of your Social Security Number (SSN) on various business-related documents, enhancing your privacy.

Applying for an EIN

The process of obtaining an EIN is straightforward and free of charge. The IRS provides several application methods: online, by fax, mail, or, for international applicants, by phone. The online application method is the fastest and most preferred. Available through the IRS website, it provides an EIN immediately upon completion of the application. The application involves filling out *Form SS-4*, which asks for details about your LLC, such as the legal name, address, and the type of tax structure you have chosen for your LLC.

If you choose to apply by fax, you must send a completed Form SS-4 to the fax number provided by the IRS for your state. This method typically sees a turnaround of about one week. For applications by mail, the process can take up to four weeks. It's crucial to ensure that all details are accurate and legible to avoid delays. Regardless of the method, it's advisable to keep a copy of your application for your records.

Uses of the EIN

Beyond its primary role in tax identification, the EIN is used in various other facets of business operations. Banks and financial institutions require an EIN to process financial documents associated with your LLC, such as loans or lines of credit. This is crucial for keeping your business and personal finances separate, a fundamental practice for legal and tax purposes.

Moreover, the EIN is required when filing your tax returns and when handling employee payroll. It must be used in all correspondence with the IRS and in all forms and invoices issued by your LLC. This consistent use helps maintain your business's tax identity and ensures that all your documents and transactions are properly traced and recorded under your business name, adding an extra layer of professionalism and credibility.

As we wrap up this chapter on forming your LLC, from the initial paperwork to obtaining your EIN, remember each step builds on the previous to create a robust framework for your business. These initial efforts lay the groundwork, ensuring your LLC is recognized legally, operates smoothly, and is prepared for future growth. In the next chapter, we will delve into managing your LLC's finances, a critical aspect to ensuring your business thrives in a competitive economic environment.

TAXATION AND FINANCIAL MANAGEMENT FOR LLCS

avigating the fiscal waters of your LLC doesn't just involve keeping your business afloat; it requires understanding the currents and undercurrents of taxation that can significantly impact your financial journey. This chapter is your compass for mastering the complex world of taxes that surround Limited Liability Companies. Here, we unfold the layers of federal, state, and local taxes, guiding you through the choices and responsibilities that define your LLC's tax status and obligations. Every dollar you save on taxes through strategic planning and compliance can be redirected towards growing your business, making tax management a critical skill for every entrepreneur.

UNDERSTANDING LLC TAXATION: FEDERAL, STATE, AND LOCAL TAXES

The taxation of Limited Liability Companies is uniquely flexible. Unlike corporations that are taxed on their income directly, LLCs enjoy what is known as "pass-through" taxation by default as mentioned in previous chapters. This means the income of the LLC is passed through to you and any other members, *and reported on your personal tax returns.* Consequently, the LLC itself does not pay taxes on its profits; instead, taxes are paid individually by the members at their personal income tax rates. This setup can have significant tax advantages, particularly in avoiding the double taxation faced by C corporations, where income is taxed once at the corporate level and again at the individual level when distributed as dividends. However, the pass-through characteristic also means that all profits are subject to income tax *in the year they are earned, whether or not these profits are distributed to members.* This can lead to tax implications that require careful financial planning to manage effectively.

While the default tax status for LLCs is pass-through, you have the flexibility to elect how your LLC is taxed. An LLC can choose to be taxed as a disregarded entity if it has only one member, as a partnership if it has two or more members, or as a corporation (either C corporation or S corporation). Each choice carries implications for tax liability and operational complexity.

1. *As a disregarded entity,* a single-member LLC is ignored for tax purposes, and all activities are reported directly on your personal tax return, akin to a sole proprietorship. This option simplifies tax filing but does not provide a payroll tax shield on earnings.
2. Being taxed *as a partnership* allows profits and losses to flow through to members' personal tax returns proportionate to their ownership interests, which offers great flexibility in business operations and tax planning.
3. Electing to be treated *as a corporation,* particularly an S corporation, can benefit members by allowing income to

be split into salaries and dividends, potentially reducing self-employment taxes. However, this option requires adherence to the standards and formalities of corporate tax rules, which can increase both your administrative burden and tax filing complexity.

State-Specific Tax Considerations

The impact of state taxes on your LLC can vary dramatically depending on where your LLC is registered and operates. Some states, like Wyoming, South Dakota, and Florida, do not impose personal income taxes, which could mean significant savings for LLC members, particularly if the LLC's income is high. Other states, like California and New York, not only impose income taxes but also levy additional franchise, business, or capital values taxes on LLCs, which can affect your business's bottom line.

Understanding the specific tax landscape of your state is essential. This includes knowing whether your state recognizes the federal S corporation election or if it imposes an entity-level tax on LLCs treated as pass-through entities. Such nuances make it crucial to either conduct thorough research or consult with a tax professional who is well-versed in the state's tax regulations.

Local Taxes

Local taxes, including city or county taxes, can often be overlooked but are just as important as federal and state taxes. Depending on your LLC's location, you may be subject to additional taxes like property taxes if your LLC owns real estate, or sales taxes, which are applicable if your LLC sells goods and services. Some localities also require specific business licenses that come with their own fees and tax implications.

To manage local taxes effectively, start by visiting your local tax authority's website or office. Many offer resources for businesses to help them understand their tax obligations. Be proactive in registering for any applicable taxes to avoid penalties and interest on late payments. Keeping abreast of the local tax requirements not only helps in maintaining compliance but also in planning your financial strategies more accurately.

By becoming well-versed in these tax obligations and strategically choosing your LLC's tax status, you can optimize your financial outcomes and ensure your business thrives in its fiscal environment. As you move forward, keep these insights in mind as they are integral to making informed decisions that align with both your business's immediate financial realities and its long-term growth objectives.

MAXIMIZING TAX BENEFITS AND DEDUCTIONS FOR YOUR LLC

Understanding how to leverage tax deductions and credits effectively can significantly enhance your financial performance. For many entrepreneurs, these deductions and credits are pivotal in reducing the overall tax burden, thereby freeing up capital that can be reinvested into the business to fuel growth and innovation. Each deduction or credit has specific qualifications and documentation requirements, and it's crucial to familiarize yourself with these to ensure you're not leaving money on the table.

One of the most common deductions for LLCs is the *business expense deduction*, which allows you to write off the costs of operating your business. This includes everyday expenses such as rent, utilities, and office supplies, as well as larger expenditures like business travel, employee salaries, and professional services fees.

To qualify for these deductions, expenses must be both ordinary (common and accepted in your field of business) and necessary (appropriate and helpful for your business). Another valuable deduction is the depreciation of assets, which covers the loss in value of larger business assets such as vehicles, furniture, and computers over their useful life.

In addition to deductions, various tax credits can reduce your tax liability directly, dollar for dollar, unlike deductions that reduce the amount of income subject to tax. For instance, the Small Business Health Care Tax Credit benefits small LLCs that provide health insurance to their employees. If you meet the eligibility criteria, including having fewer than 25 full-time equivalent employees and paying an average wage below a certain threshold, you can claim up to 50% of the premiums paid.

For strategic tax planning, it's advantageous to think beyond the current year. Effective tax strategies involve a thorough understanding of potential future changes in tax laws and adjusting your business operations accordingly. For example, if new tax legislation is introduced that offers benefits for investments in renewable energy, you might consider how incorporating green technologies into your business operations could not only reduce your tax liability but also enhance your brand's reputation and operational efficiency.

Maintaining meticulous records is non-negotiable when it comes to claiming deductions and preparing for audits. Proper documentation supports the expenses claimed on your tax returns, and having organized records can expedite the audit process and resolve questions from the IRS more quickly. Use dedicated business accounting software to track expenses as they occur, store receipts digitally, and keep detailed logs of business travel and vehicle use. This rigorous approach to record-keeping not only supports your tax filing but also provides you with insights into your business's financial health, informing better decision-making.

- **Case Study: Tech Startup Maximizes R&D Tax Credit**

Consider the case of a burgeoning tech startup specializing in educational software. In its early years, the company invested heavily in research and development (R&D), a common expenditure for startups aiming to bring innovative products to market. However, the financial strain of these investments was significant. After consulting with a tax professional, the startup began claiming the R&D Tax Credit, designed to encourage businesses to invest in innovation within the U.S.

By meticulously documenting their development processes, employee hours spent on R&D, and associated costs, the startup was able to claim a substantial tax credit, which significantly offset its tax liability. This strategic move not only alleviated financial pressure but also enabled the startup to reinvest the savings into further innovation and market expansion. This example underscores the importance of understanding the specific tax credits available to your industry and maintaining detailed records that can substantiate your claims.

Navigating the complexities of taxes may not be the most exhilarating part of entrepreneurship, but with a strategic approach to leveraging deductions and credits, effective tax planning can become a powerful tool in enhancing your LLC's profitability and sustainability.

FINANCIAL RECORD-KEEPING: BEST PRACTICES FOR LLCS

Setting up an effective accounting system is akin to laying down the nervous system for your LLC—it channels vital information to where it's needed, ensuring the health and efficiency of your business operations. As an entrepreneur, understanding the nuts and bolts of setting up these systems is crucial not just for compliance, but for gaining insights into your business's financial health. The first step in establishing a robust accounting system is choosing the right software that fits the needs of your LLC. This choice will largely depend on the size of your business, the complexity of your financial transactions, and your budget. For most small to medium-sized LLCs, cloud-based accounting software like *QuickBooks Online*, *Xero*, or *FreshBooks* is suitable. These platforms offer the flexibility of accessing your financial data from anywhere, provide automatic updates, and scale with your business as it grows.

When implementing your accounting system, it's essential to customize it to the specific needs of your LLC. This involves setting up appropriate account categories that reflect your business operations, such as sales, supplies, payroll, and taxes. Properly categorizing transactions from the outset helps in maintaining orderly records and simplifies the process of financial review and reporting. Additionally, integrating your accounting software with other tools like your point-of-sale system, payroll services, and bank accounts can automate data entries, reduce errors, and save time. Once your system is set up, training is crucial. Ensure that you and your team understand how to use the accounting software effectively. Regular training sessions can help in staying updated with new features and best practices, ensuring that your financial data is handled accurately and securely.

Maintaining accurate financial records is not a one-off task but a continuous commitment that requires diligence and regularity. Daily financial tasks such as recording transactions, reviewing and reconciling bank statements, and managing invoices and receipts are fundamental in keeping your financial records up to date. This daily discipline prevents the pile-up of unrecorded transactions, which can lead to confusion and errors in your financial statements. Monthly tasks are equally important; they include reviewing past-due receivables, reconciling all accounts, and preparing monthly financial reports. These reports, which typically comprise the *profit and loss statement, balance sheet,* and *cash flow statement,* provide a snapshot of your business's financial health and are essential for making informed business decisions.

Long-term financial planning is where strategic thinking comes into play, blending foresight with your current financial data to steer your business towards growth and stability. Developing a financial forecast as part of your long-term planning involves analyzing past financial data and market conditions to make educated predictions about future income, expenses, and cash flow. This forecast allows you to anticipate financial needs, such as funding for expansion or new hires, and to plan accordingly. It also provides a benchmark against which to measure your business's performance over time. Budgeting, a core component of financial planning, helps in managing your finances proactively. It involves creating a plan for how your business will spend its resources to reach its goals. Regularly comparing your actual financial results with your budgeted figures can highlight where your business is over or under-performing, allowing you to make necessary adjustments.

Using financial data to make informed business decisions is arguably the most impactful practice in managing your LLC. Financial data offers critical insights into aspects like which products or services are most profitable, which marketing strategies are yielding a good return on investment, and where cost reductions can be made without impacting product quality. For instance, if your financial data shows a consistently high cost for certain materials, you might consider seeking alternative suppliers or negotiating better terms with current suppliers. Similarly, if certain products or services are not profitable, you might decide to discontinue them or adjust pricing strategies. The key is to use the data not just for routine financial management but as a strategic tool to drive your business decisions.

In essence, setting up and maintaining an effective accounting system, coupled with diligent record-keeping and strategic financial planning, provides the foundation for not just surviving in the competitive business landscape but thriving. As you continue to integrate these practices into your daily operations, they become less of a chore and more of a pivotal part of your business strategy, driving efficiency, clarity, and growth in your entrepreneurial endeavors.

NAVIGATING SELF-EMPLOYMENT TAXES AND PAYROLL FOR LLCS

Navigating the nuances of self-employment taxes and setting up a systematic payroll can seem daunting, but with the right information and tools, it becomes a manageable part of running your LLC. Self-employment taxes are a fundamental aspect of fiscal responsibility for any LLC owner who actively participates in the business. These taxes contribute to your coverage under the social security system, providing you with retirement benefits, disability benefits, and Medicare eligibility. Essentially, when you work as an employee, these contributions are split between you and your employer. However, as a self-employed individual, you handle both portions, which is why understanding how these taxes are calculated and when they are due is crucial.

Self-employment taxes are based on the net earnings of your business. This means they are calculated after deducting business expenses from your gross income. For 2024, the self-employment tax rate is 15.3%, comprising 12.4% for social security and 2.9% for Medicare. There is a cap on the social security portion, which is adjusted annually; however, the Medicare portion applies to all your *net earnings*. To manage these taxes effectively, it is advisable to set aside a portion of your net earnings regularly so that you are prepared when it's time to pay these taxes, typically each quarter through estimated tax payments.

When it comes to payroll, if your LLC has employees, setting up a structured payroll system is not just a convenience; it's a legal requirement. The first step in establishing a payroll system is to obtain an Employer Identification Number (EIN) from the IRS, if you haven't already done so when setting up your LLC. This will be used to report taxes and other documents to the IRS and the state agency. Next, you need to decide on a pay period—whether it will be weekly, biweekly, or monthly. This decision might be influenced by state laws, as some states require at least bi-monthly pay periods for employees.

Additionally, you must understand and manage withholding taxes, which include federal income tax, state and local taxes, and contributions to social security and Medicare. Calculating the correct amount to withhold can be complex, depending on each employee's filing status and allowances claimed on their W-4 form. Therefore, using reliable payroll software or hiring a payroll service provider can be highly beneficial. These services not only calculate taxes and generate paychecks but also handle tax filings and year-end forms like W-2s, reducing the likelihood of errors and ensuring compliance.

The distinction between *owner draws* and *payroll distributions* is another critical area for LLCs, particularly those that choose to be taxed as an S corporation. In such cases, if you are an owner actively working in the business, the IRS requires you to pay yourself a reasonable salary before taking any additional distributions. This salary must be comparable to what someone in a similar position would earn in another company. Paying a reasonable salary means that the appropriate amount of payroll taxes are paid on these earnings, which is crucial as the IRS scrutinizes these distributions to prevent owners from avoiding payroll taxes by taking money out of the business only as distributions.

One common pitfall in managing self-employment taxes and payroll is the failure to keep accurate records and to separate personal and business expenses. This can lead to under or over-calculating your tax obligations. To avoid this, ensure all business transactions are conducted through a business bank account and meticulously track all business expenses and income. This practice not only aids in accurate tax calculation but also simplifies the process of filing your tax returns.

Another frequent error is not making estimated tax payments throughout the year. This oversight can lead to unexpected large tax bills and potential penalties at year-end. Setting up a routine where you regularly set aside money for taxes in a separate bank account can help manage these payments effectively. Remember, paying these taxes is not just about compliance; it's about ensuring that you remain in good standing with the tax authorities and avoiding any disruptions to your business operations.

By understanding and effectively managing self-employment taxes and payroll, you place your LLC on a firm footing, legally and financially. With systems in place to handle these fundamental aspects, you can focus more on growing your business and less on navigating tax complexities. This proactive approach not only ensures compliance but fosters a structured environment where both you and your employees can thrive.

ESSENTIAL FINANCIAL TOOLS AND SOFTWARE FOR LLC MANAGEMENT

In the digital age, the right financial tools and software are not just conveniences—they are essential components that can significantly enhance the efficiency and accuracy of your LLC's financial management. The landscape of available financial software is vast, but choosing the right tools that fit the specific needs of your business can transform the way you handle everything from daily bookkeeping to long-term financial planning. This section offers a deep dive into the various software options tailored for small businesses and LLCs, helping you make informed decisions that streamline your financial operations.

When considering accounting software, the sheer variety of options can seem overwhelming, but focusing on solutions that are tailored to small businesses can narrow down the choices. Popular platforms like *QuickBooks Online, Xero, and Sage Business Cloud Accounting* stand out due to their comprehensive features that cater specifically to small business needs. These platforms offer robust functionalities including invoicing, expense tracking, payroll processing, and financial reporting. Each software comes with its unique strengths; *QuickBooks Online* is renowned for its extensive ecosystem and integration capabilities, making it a versatile choice for businesses that use multiple apps. *Xero* offers strong collaboration features which are ideal if you have a team managing your finances, while *Sage Business Cloud Accounting* is known for its strong compliance features, making it suitable for businesses that need to meet specific industry standards.

For many small business owners, managing bookkeeping without a dedicated finance team is a reality. In such cases, software like *FreshBooks* offers a user-friendly interface and simple navigation which can be particularly beneficial. It also integrates seamlessly with a range of other tools such as email platforms, customer relationship management software, and more, streamlining your operations. Another excellent option is *Wave*, which provides free basic bookkeeping features along with additional paid services. This can be a great starting point if you're keeping a tight rein on expenses but want a software that can scale with your business.

Discussing the benefits of integrating your accounting software with other business tools, the efficiencies gained cannot be over-stated. Integration allows for the automatic transfer of data across platforms, reducing the need for manual data entry, which can be both time-consuming and prone to errors. For example, integrating your accounting software with your e-commerce platform can automatically record sales data, streamlining revenue tracking and inventory management. Similarly, integration with payment gateways can facilitate smoother transaction processing, ensuring that your financial records are always up-to-date and accurate. These integrations not only save time but also provide real-time financial data, which is crucial for making timely business decisions.

Security considerations are paramount when selecting financial tools and software. The sensitivity of financial data means that the security features of your software are not just a technicality but a necessity. When evaluating options, look for features like two-factor authentication, end-to-end encryption, and regular security audits. Additionally, consider the software's compliance with regulations such as the General Data Protection Regulation (GDPR) if you operate in or have dealings with entities in the European Union. Ensuring that your financial data is secure from unauthorized access is crucial not only for your peace of mind but also for maintaining the trust of your customers and partners.

Lastly, customizing tools to fit the specific needs of your LLC can greatly enhance their effectiveness. Many software platforms offer the option to add modules or integrations as your business grows, so you can start with a basic setup and expand your tools as your needs develop. By selecting software that aligns well with your operational requirements and financial management style, you can establish a robust framework that supports efficient and secure financial management, freeing up more of your time to focus on growing your business.

PLANNING FOR THE FUTURE: TAXES AND YOUR LLC

In the ever-evolving landscape of business, proactive tax strategies are not just about compliance and saving money; they're about securing the future of your LLC. The forward-thinking entrepreneur views tax planning through a long-term lens, anticipating changes and positioning the business to capitalize on potential tax advantages. This strategic approach not only minimizes current tax liabilities but also sets the foundation for sustainable growth and continuity.

Long-Term Tax Strategies

Optimizing your tax situation means more than just reacting to yearly tax obligations; it involves setting up strategies that benefit your financial health over the long haul. One effective strategy is deferring income to the next tax year while accelerating deductions into the current year, which can reduce taxable income and the corresponding tax liability. This might involve timing the purchase of business equipment to coincide with the end of the fiscal year or delaying invoicing for services until the new tax year begins. Another long-term strategy is to structure your business to make the most of tax credits and incentives that encourage specific activities, such as hiring from certain demographics, investing in research and development, or implementing eco-friendly improvements to your business operations.

For LLCs looking to grow or even maintain flexibility in their business structure, considering the tax implications of different business formations can lead to significant tax savings. For example, electing to be taxed as an S corporation might make sense as your business grows and profits increase, potentially saving on self-employment taxes by allowing you to split your income between salary and distributions. These decisions should align with both your current financial scenario and your long-term business goals, balancing the complexity and potential benefits of various tax strategies. We'll discuss more about S Corporation in Chapter 8.

Succession Planning and Taxes

The continuity of your LLC is a critical consideration that can be significantly impacted by tax planning, especially in the context of succession planning. As you plan for the future, whether it involves passing the business to an heir or selling it, understanding the tax implications of these transitions is essential. For example, the structure of your LLC can affect how it is transferred. If your LLC is sold, the tax implications can vary based on whether it is a sale of assets or a sale of membership interests, each with different tax treatments and consequences.

Implementing a robust succession plan that includes tax-efficient strategies for transferring ownership can prevent unexpected tax burdens that might otherwise jeopardize the business's financial stability during the transition phase. Strategies such as gifting portions of the business over time to heirs or setting up buy-sell agreements funded with life insurance can ensure not only a smoother transition but also a tax-efficient one.

Building a Relationship with a Tax Professional

Perhaps one of the most impactful actions you can take for your LLC's financial health is to cultivate a lasting relationship with a tax professional who understands the nuances of your business. A skilled tax advisor does more than ensure compliance; they can provide strategic advice that aligns with your business goals and adapts to the changing tax landscape. This relationship can be a cornerstone of your business's financial strategy, providing clarity amidst the complexities of tax planning and ongoing financial management.

A tax professional who is familiar with your business can tailor their advice to your specific circumstances, helping you to make informed decisions that balance tax efficiency with business growth and stability. They can become a trusted advisor whose insights contribute to strategic decisions, from daily operations to long-term planning. This partnership not only enhances your ability to navigate tax complexities but also enriches your strategic planning with expert insights, driving better financial outcomes for your LLC.

As we conclude this exploration of future-focused tax planning for your LLC, remember that the strategies discussed here are not just about meeting legal obligations—they are about setting your business up for future success. By integrating these tax strategies into your broader business planning, you ensure that your LLC is positioned to thrive in the changing economic landscape, backed by a solid plan that anticipates and adapts to changes. As we move forward, the next chapter will delve into the legal intricacies of running your LLC, ensuring that your business is not only financially sound but also legally robust. This natural progression from financial foresight to legal diligence will equip you with the comprehensive knowledge necessary to navigate the complexities of business ownership.

DAY-TO-DAY LLC OPERATIONS

$\mathcal{N}$avigating the daily operations of your LLC involves more than just overseeing the workflow and managing projects; it demands a meticulous approach to the financial health and legal compliance of your business. This chapter delves into the backbone of your LLC's operational success—effective bookkeeping and accounting practices. Whether you're a solo entrepreneur or leading a growing team, mastering these financial disciplines will ensure your business not only survives the competitive marketplace but thrives within it.

EFFECTIVE BOOKKEEPING STRATEGIES FOR LLC OWNERS

The cornerstone of sound financial management in any business, especially in an LLC, is maintaining *a regular and robust book-keeping routine*. Bookkeeping goes beyond mere record-keeping; it involves systematically recording, organizing, and analyzing every financial transaction your business makes. Regularity in this process ensures that you not only keep track of every dollar that flows in and out of your business but also remain compliant with tax laws and regulations that require detailed financial records.

Consider setting aside a specific time each week or month dedicated solely to updating your books. This could involve reconciling bank statements with your internal records, capturing receipts and logging expenses, or reviewing accounts receivable to ensure invoices are paid promptly. The consistency of this routine helps in early detection of discrepancies that could indicate deeper issues like cash flow problems or even fraudulent activities. Moreover, it ensures that come tax season, you are not overwhelmed with the task of organizing a year's worth of financial data, which can be both time-consuming and fraught with errors if done in haste.

Understanding Financial Statements

For many new entrepreneurs, financial statements can seem like daunting documents filled with figures and financial jargon. However, these statements—the *balance sheet, income statement,* and *cash flow statement*—are vital tools that offer insights into your business's financial health and trajectory.

1. *The balance sheet* provides a snapshot of your company's financial standing at a specific point in time. It lists all of your LLC's assets, liabilities, and equity, and helps you understand what your business owns and owes.

2. *The income statement,* or *profit and loss statement,* shows your business's performance over a period. It

details revenues, expenses, and profits or losses, giving you a clear picture of your operational success.

3. **The cash flow statement** tracks the flow of cash in and out of your business, offering a view of how well you manage cash for operational needs, financing activities, and investments.

Learning to generate and interpret these statements allows you to make informed decisions about cost-cutting, investments, and growth strategies. For instance, a dip in cash flow might prompt you to tighten credit terms with customers or seek better payment terms with suppliers. Regular review of these statements can also help you spot trends, prepare for future financial needs, and communicate more effectively with financial advisors and potential investors.

Hiring a Professional

While many small business owners start out handling book-keeping on their own, there comes a point when hiring a professional bookkeeper or accountant can be a wise investment. If you find that managing your books is taking up too much of your time, preventing you from focusing on growing your business, or if your financial transactions have become too complex, it might be time to bring in a professional.

An *experienced bookkeeper* can manage day-to-day financial recording and ensure your books are always up-to-date and accurately reflect your business's financial activities. An *accountant* can take this a step further by offering strategic financial advice, assisting with tax planning, and preparing detailed financial reports. These professionals not only help maintain financial order but can also provide insights that lead to cost savings and business opportunities, potentially offsetting their costs.

Moreover, the peace of mind that comes from knowing your financial records are in expert hands—and that you are consistently compliant with relevant laws and regulations—can be invaluable. This is particularly crucial in an LLC, where financial mismanagement can not only result in legal repercussions but also impact your personal liability protection.

Incorporating these bookkeeping strategies into your daily operations is not just about keeping good financial records; it's about creating a system that supports your business's operational efficiency, compliance, and growth. As you continue to integrate these practices, you'll find they provide not just clarity and control over your finances but also contribute significantly to your business's ongoing success and stability.

MANAGING LLC CASH FLOW: TIPS AND TRICKS

Understanding and managing your LLC's cash flow is akin to navigating a river; it requires keen attention to the currents and undercurrents to ensure a smooth journey. Effective cash flow management is not just about monitoring the money entering and exiting your business; it's about strategizing and optimizing these flows to maintain a healthy financial state. This section guides you through the critical aspects of cash flow analysis, enhancing receivables, controlling expenses, and the strategic importance of maintaining an emergency fund.

Cash flow analysis starts with a clear understanding of where your money comes from and where it goes. This process involves reviewing your financial transactions and categorizing them to identify trends and patterns. For instance, you might notice that your cash inflows peak during certain months or that certain expenses recur regularly. By mapping out these patterns, you can forecast future cash flows with greater accuracy. This forecasting allows you to anticipate periods of cash surplus or shortage, enabling you to make informed decisions such as when to invest in new assets or increase marketing efforts. To effectively analyze your cash flow, utilize tools like cash flow statements and projections that offer a detailed view of your finances over a specific period. These tools help you visualize not only your current financial status but also simulate various business scenarios to see how they might affect your cash flow. For example, you can assess how increasing payment terms from 30 to 45 days might impact your liquidity.

Improving receivables is crucial in enhancing your cash inflow, ensuring you have enough cash on hand to meet your business obligations. Effective strategies include tightening your credit policies, offering early payment discounts, and implementing more efficient invoicing procedures. For example, automating your invoicing process can significantly reduce the time between providing a service and issuing an invoice, thereby speeding up payments. Consider using online invoicing services that allow you to send invoices immediately and include convenient payment options for your customers. Additionally, regularly reviewing your accounts receivable to identify and address late payments promptly can prevent cash flow disruptions. Communicating clearly and promptly with clients about their payment statuses and any overdue balances, possibly offering payment plans for larger bills, can also encourage quicker payments and strengthen client relationships.

Controlling expenses is another vital aspect of managing cash flow. Regular review and justification of all expenses can help you identify areas where you can cut costs without compromising the quality of your goods or services. This might involve renegotiating contracts with suppliers, opting for cost-effective marketing strategies, or implementing energy-saving measures to reduce utility bills. Adopting a zero-based budgeting approach where every expense must be justified for each new period can also help in maintaining tight control over outflows. Moreover, continuously seeking feedback from your team can uncover insights into areas where processes can be optimized or where wastage can be reduced, further helping in expense control. Monitoring your cash flow patterns might also reveal less obvious areas of savings, such as adjusting inventory levels to match sales patterns, thereby reducing holding costs.

Finally, the importance of *maintaining an emergency fund* cannot be overstated. This fund acts as a financial safety net that can help your business weather unexpected financial challenges such as a sudden drop in sales, urgent repairs, or economic downturns. The size of this fund will vary depending on your business size, industry, and cash flow stability, but having at least three to six months' worth of operating expenses is generally recommended. To build your emergency fund, set aside a small portion of your monthly income, treating it as a non-negotiable expense. This proactive approach not only secures your business against unforeseen circumstances but also provides peace of mind, allowing you to focus on growth and expansion opportunities.

By integrating these strategies into your financial management practices, you can enhance your LLC's ability to generate positive cash flow, reduce financial stress, and create a buffer that supports business stability and growth.

THE ROLE OF DIGITAL MARKETING IN GROWING YOUR LLC

In today's tech-savvy environment, digital marketing is not just an option but a crucial element in the growth and sustainability of any business, including your LLC. Initiating a robust digital marketing strategy allows you to connect with a broader audience, engage with customers more effectively, and enhance your brand's visibility online. Let's explore how to craft a digital marketing plan that aligns with your LLC's objectives and resonates with your target audience.

Developing a comprehensive digital marketing strategy begins with a clear understanding of your business goals and the specific needs of your audience. Start by defining what you aim to achieve through digital marketing—be it increasing brand awareness, boosting sales, or enhancing customer engagement. Each goal will dictate different tactics and platforms, making this initial clarity essential. Next, delve into understanding your target audience; knowing their preferences, online behavior, and content consumption patterns will allow you to tailor your marketing efforts more effectively. With these insights, you can then choose the right digital channels—whether it's social media, email marketing, or your business website—to reach your audience effectively. The next step involves setting up measurable objectives, such as a specific number of new leads or a percentage increase in website traffic, which will help you gauge the success of your marketing efforts. Finally, plan your resources—both budget and manpower—needed to execute your strategy. This comprehensive planning ensures that your digital marketing efforts are structured, focused, and aligned with your business's overall objectives.

Moving into the realm of *content marketing*, the power of compelling and relevant content cannot be overstated. Content marketing focuses on creating and distributing relevant content that is key to attract and retain a clearly-defined audience — ultimately driving profitable customer action. Start by identifying the types of content that will appeal to your target audience, which could range from blog posts and articles to videos and podcasts. The goal is to provide your audience with content will solve their problems, educates them, or even entertains them, thereby building trust and establishing your brand as an authority in your field. For instance, if your LLC sells eco-friendly products, you could produce content about sustainability practices, how-to guides on using your products, and the benefits of choosing eco-friendly options. This not only informs your audience but also aligns with your brand's values. Remember, consistency in your content delivery helps keep your audience engaged and encourages them to return to your platforms, increasing the likelihood of conversion from viewer to customer.

In today's digital age, your online visibility can significantly impact your business growth, and this is where Search Engine Optimization (SEO) comes into play. SEO involves optimizing your website and its content to rank higher in search engine results pages. Begin with keyword research to understand the terms and phrases your target audience uses when searching for products or services like yours. Incorporate these keywords strategically in your website's content, meta descriptions, and even in the alt text of images. However, SEO is not just about keywords; ensuring your website is mobile-friendly, improves page loading times, and provides a good user experience are all critical factors that affect your SEO rankings. Regularly updating your content and ensuring it provides value to your readers also signals to search engines that your website is a relevant and authoritative source, boosting your SEO efforts.

Finally, understanding and measuring the success of your digital marketing efforts is crucial to refining your strategies and achieving your business goals. Utilize analytics tools to track your performance across various digital platforms. Tools like Google Analytics can provide comprehensive data on your website's traffic, user behavior, and conversion rates. Social media platforms also offer insights into the performance of your posts and audience engagement. By regularly reviewing these metrics, you can identify what's working and what's not, allowing you to adjust your strategies for better results. For instance, if you notice that video content generates more engagement on your social media platforms, you might decide to allocate more resources to video production. Conversely, if certain types of content or campaigns are not performing well, you can either modify them or reallocate your budget to more effective tactics.

Incorporating these elements into your digital marketing efforts will not only enhance your online presence but also drive tangible growth for your LLC. As you continue to adapt and refine your strategies based on performance data and changing market trends, your digital marketing initiatives will remain a pivotal aspect of your business's success in the digital landscape.

LEVERAGING SOCIAL MEDIA FOR BUSINESS DEVELOPMENT

In the dynamic landscape of modern business, social media stands as a pivotal platform for building and expanding your LLC's reach and influence. The choice of social media platforms, however, should align closely with your business goals and the specific demographics of your target audience. Different platforms cater to varied audience types and offer distinct advantages depending on your business's nature. For instance, if your LLC is in the fashion or lifestyle sector, visually-oriented platforms like Instagram and Pinterest could be highly beneficial due to their image-centric content which allows for high engagement through visual posts. On the other hand, if your focus is on B2B services, LinkedIn might be more appropriate because of its professional network base, providing opportunities to connect with other businesses and industry professionals.

Choosing the right platform goes beyond just identifying where your audience spends their time; it involves understanding the unique features and advertising algorithms of each platform and how they can be leveraged to meet your business objectives. For example, Facebook offers extensive market segmentation tools that allow you to target specific demographics, making it an excellent platform for tailored marketing campaigns. Twitter, with its rapid and concise communication style, is ideal for businesses that rely on timely updates or engagements, such as media companies or tech businesses.

Building a robust social media presence is vital for cultivating an engaging brand image and fostering loyalty among your followers. Start by creating compelling, high-quality content that resonates with your audience. This could range from informative articles and exciting updates to interactive content like polls or live Q&As, which drive engagement and encourage participation. Consistency in your posting schedule also helps keep your audience engaged while giving your business a dependable and professional image. Employing a consistent brand voice and visual style across all your posts helps reinforce your brand identity, making your content immediately recognizable to your audience. This consistency should reflect your brand's values and promise, whether it's professionalism, creativity, friendliness, or innovation.

As you enhance your social media presence, consider the strategic use of social media advertising to broaden your reach and improve engagement. Social media platforms offer powerful tools for targeted advertising that can significantly increase your visibility and attract new followers. These tools allow you to target users based on a myriad of factors including age, interests, behavior, and more, ensuring that your marketing efforts reach the most relevant audience. Budgeting for social media advertising should be a thoughtful process; start small to test what works best for your business before scaling up. Tracking the performance of your ads in real-time allows you to adjust your strategy and budget allocation to maximize ROI.

The final pillar of a successful social media strategy is fostering engagement and building a community around your brand. Engagement on social media isn't just about counting likes and shares; it's about creating meaningful interactions that foster a sense of community and loyalty. Encourage your followers to interact with your content through calls-to-action, ask questions to spark discussions, and respond promptly to comments and messages to build a rapport with your audience. Hosting regular events on social media, such as webinars, contests, or live sessions, can also keep your audience engaged and give them a reason to keep coming back. Moreover, listening to your audience's feedback on social media can provide invaluable insights into their preferences and perceptions, which can be leveraged to improve your products or services.

Implementing these strategies in your social media efforts can transform your platforms from mere broadcasting channels into dynamic spaces for interaction and growth. By meticulously choosing the right platforms, crafting engaging content, strategically investing in advertising, and actively fostering community engagement, your LLC can tap into the vast potential of social media to expand its reach and solidify its presence in the market. As you continue to adapt and evolve these strategies in response to changing trends and audience behaviors, your social media platforms will remain a vital asset in your business development toolkit.

ESSENTIAL TECH TOOLS FOR LLC PRODUCTIVITY

In the fast-paced world of business, leveraging the right technology can dramatically enhance your LLC's operational efficiency and productivity. The market is flush with software tools designed to streamline various aspects of business management, from project coordination to time tracking, each serving a unique purpose in bolstering your company's productivity landscape. Delving into productivity software, tools like *Asana* and *Trello* stand out for their robust project management capabilities. These platforms allow you to organize tasks, set deadlines, and update statuses in a visually intuitive interface. This can be particularly beneficial for managing multiple projects simultaneously, ensuring that nothing slips through the cracks. For time tracking, apps like *Toggl* and *Harvest* offer simple yet powerful solutions to monitor how much time is spent on various tasks. This not only aids in productivity analysis but also enhances time management across your team, ensuring that key projects receive the attention they deserve without overshooting budgets.

Automation tools offer another layer of efficiency by handling repetitive tasks that can consume a disproportionate amount of time. For instance, *Zapier* automates workflows by connecting over 1,000 apps, enabling automatic data transfer between platforms without manual intervention. This can be a game-changer for tasks such as updating customer records, posting on social media, or aggregating data for reports. Automating these tasks reduces the likelihood of human error and frees up your team to focus on more strategic activities that require human insight and creativity. Another powerful tool in this category is *IFTTT* (If This Then That), which creates conditional statements, or "applets," that automate interactions between apps and devices. For example, you can create an applet that automatically saves attachments from emails to a designated Dropbox folder, streamlining file management and ensuring important documents are always accessible.

In today's increasingly remote work environment, collaboration tools have become indispensable for maintaining team cohesion and ensuring seamless communication. *Slack*, a platform that organizes team communication into channels, stands out for its ease of use and integration capabilities. It allows your team to stay connected, share files, and manage tasks in real-time, regardless of physical location. For video conferencing, tools like *Zoom* and *Microsoft Teams* not only facilitate virtual meetings but also offer features like screen sharing, virtual backgrounds, and real-time collaboration on documents. These functionalities ensure that team interactions remain dynamic and productive, mimicking the immediacy of in-person collaboration as closely as possible.

Lastly, the critical aspect of data security must be underscored, as the integrity and confidentiality of your business information are paramount. Implementing robust data security tools and practices is essential to protect sensitive information from cyber threats. Tools like *Bitdefender* or *Norton* provide comprehensive security solutions that include virus protection, firewall, online transaction protection, and more. Additionally, employing practices such as regular software updates, strong password policies, and multi-factor authentication can significantly enhance your defense against cyber attacks. A data breach can be costly, not just financially but also in terms of customer trust and business reputation, making investment in good security practices a wise decision for any business, especially in an era where data breaches are becoming more common.

By integrating these essential tech tools into your LLC's operations, you not only boost productivity but also foster a work environment that is efficient, secure, and adaptable to the demands of modern business.

BUILDING YOUR TEAM: HIRING EMPLOYEES AND CONTRACTORS

Building a strong team is pivotal to the success of your LLC, whether you're bringing on full-time employees or engaging contractors for specific projects. The process involves strategic planning to ensure that each team member aligns with your business objectives and enhances your operational capacity. Let's navigate through effective recruitment strategies, establishing a thorough onboarding process, managing remote workers, and understanding the legalities of hiring.

When recruiting, attracting the right talent involves a blend of clear communication about your company's vision and the roles you need to fill, alongside a keen understanding of the market for talent. Begin by crafting job descriptions that not only detail the responsibilities and requirements of the position but also high-light the culture and core values of your LLC. This transparency helps in attracting candidates who not only have the skills but also share the values of your business, fostering a better long-term fit. Utilize a variety of platforms to advertise your openings —from popular job boards and industry-specific websites to social media and professional networking sites like LinkedIn. Diversifying your recruitment channels broadens your reach and increases the likelihood of discovering top talent.

Moreover, consider implementing creative recruitment strategies such as hosting open house events, participating in industry conferences, or offering internships. These approaches not only widen your talent pool but also give potential candidates a real-life glimpse into your business environment, which can be a powerful persuader. It's also beneficial to leverage your existing networks; sometimes the best recommendations come through word-of-mouth from trusted colleagues or business associates.

Once you've attracted the right candidates and made your hires, a well-structured onboarding process is crucial for seamless inte-gration into your team. Onboarding is more than just a series of introductions; it's a comprehensive process that should equip new hires with the tools and information they need to perform their roles effectively. Start by setting clear milestones for the first 30, 60, and 90 days, which can include goals like mastering specific tools, understanding company workflows, or completing key projects. Pairing new hires with a mentor or a peer buddy can also ease their transition by providing them with a go-to person for questions and guidance.

During onboarding, ensure that new team members understand your business's mission, strategic goals, and culture. This might involve presentations from different departments, participation in key meetings, or immersive sessions on company history and future aspirations. Remember, effective onboarding should foster a sense of belonging and provide clarity on how individual roles contribute to the broader business objectives, which enhances job satisfaction and productivity.

Managing a team that includes remote workers presents unique challenges, particularly in maintaining communication and ensuring everyone stays on task. Utilize digital tools such as Slack, Microsoft Teams, or Asana to keep communication lines open and projects on track. Regular video conferences can also help in maintaining personal connections and ensuring that remote team members feel as engaged and valued as those in the office. Establish clear expectations around availability and response times and use shared calendars to keep everyone informed of deadlines and important meetings. It's also important to cultivate a culture that respects work-life boundaries to prevent burnout—a common risk in remote work settings.

Finally, it's essential to be cognizant of the legal considerations when hiring. This includes understanding the distinctions between employees and contractors, as this impacts how you handle taxes and compliance with labor laws. Employees typically require you to withhold income tax and pay Social Security, Medicare taxes, and unemployment tax on wages paid. In contrast, contractors handle their own tax obligations, but it's crucial to correctly classify workers to avoid penalties. Ensure employment contracts are meticulously drafted to outline roles, responsibilities, compensation, and termination conditions. Staying informed about employment laws in your jurisdiction and consulting with a legal professional can help mitigate risks and ensure compliance.

As you implement these strategies in building your team, remember that each employee or contractor you bring on board is not just filling a role but is also a potential catalyst for innovation and growth in your LLC. By investing time and resources into effective hiring and management practices, you create a dynamic team environment that drives your business forward.

Transitioning from the internal dynamics of team management, the next chapter will explore the external aspects of fostering partnerships and professional relationships that further enhance your LLC's potential for growth and success. By understanding how to effectively navigate both internal and external business relationships, you lay a dual foundation for robust business operations and strategic market positioning.

LEGAL COMPLIANCE AND RISK MANAGEMENT

*N*avigating the waters of legal compliance and risk management can sometimes feel like charting a course through uncharted territory. As an entrepreneur, your ability to steer clear of potential legal pitfalls while ensuring that your business complies with applicable laws and regulations is not just beneficial—it's imperative. This chapter aims to equip you with the tools and knowledge needed to maintain your LLC's legal health, ensuring that your business operations flow smoothly and are shielded from avoidable legal complications.

REPORTS AND OTHER COMPLIANCE REQUIREMENTS

Filing Annual Reports: The Backbone of Your LLC's Compliance

The annual report for an LLC is not just a formality—it's a critical legal document that keeps your business in good standing with the state. This report typically includes essential information about your LLC, such as the names and addresses of members and managers, the principal business address, and sometimes details about your business activities over the past year. The requirements can vary significantly from state to state, both in terms of the information required and the deadlines for submission, but the core purpose remains the same: to keep the state updated on your LLC's status and to renew your right to operate legally within its borders.

Filing your annual report may seem like a bureaucratic chore, but it plays a vital role in your business's lifecycle. Failure to file can lead to penalties, fines, or even administrative dissolution of your LLC, which can disrupt your operations and damage your business's credibility. To manage this process effectively, mark the filing deadlines on your calendar as recurring events, and consider setting reminders a few weeks in advance to gather any necessary information and complete the filing without rush. Many states now offer online filing, which can simplify the process significantly. Taking the time once a year to ensure this critical task is completed can save you a multitude of headaches and keep your business on a steady course.

Renewing Licenses and Permits: Keeping Your Business Legitimately Operational

Just as your driver's license needs regular renewal to keep you legally behind the wheel, your business licenses and permits require timely updates to keep your LLC operational. Whether it's a general business operation license, a professional license, or specific permits related to health and safety, staying on top of renewal deadlines is essential. The types of licenses and permits your LLC needs can vary based on your industry, location, and the size of your operation, making it crucial to understand and comply with local, state, and federal requirements.

Consider creating a compliance calendar that includes all renewal dates, associated costs, and any prerequisites for renewal, such as inspections or continuing education credits. This proactive approach not only ensures that you remain compliant but also helps in budgeting for the costs associated with these renewals, avoiding any surprises that could disrupt your business budget or operations. Regularly reviewing your required licenses and permits can also alert you to any changes in legislation that might affect your business, allowing you to adapt and respond effectively.

Record-Keeping for Compliance: The Art of Organized Documentation

Effective record-keeping is the cornerstone of legal compliance for any LLC. Maintaining comprehensive records is not merely about organization—it's a legal requirement that supports your business's operational integrity and compliance with tax laws and regulatory statutes. Essential records include your LLC's formation documents, financial records, tax filings, annual reports, licenses and permits, employee records, and minutes of meetings. Each type of record has its own retention timeline, dictated by state laws or federal regulations.

To manage your records effectively, consider using a digital record-keeping system that allows for easy storage, access, and retrieval of documents. Cloud-based solutions can offer secure, scalable options for storing sensitive business documents, while also facilitating compliance with data protection regulations. Regular audits of your records can ensure that everything is up-to-date and archived according to legal standards, and can be invaluable during tax season, in the event of legal disputes, or when dealing with regulatory inspections.

INTELLECTUAL PROPERTY CONSIDERATIONS FOR YOUR LLC

Understanding and protecting the intellectual property (IP) of your LLC is not just a legal necessity; it's a strategic business move that can significantly enhance your market position and revenue. Intellectual property can include a variety of creations from your business—everything from logos and brand names to inventions, written content, and even proprietary processes. Recognizing the types of IP your business holds is the first step toward leveraging these assets for competitive advantage. For instance, if your LLC has developed a unique product, the design or specific technology used could be considered a patentable invention. Similarly, any logos or designs that are central to your brand identity could be protected as trademarks.

Once you've identified potential IP within your LLC, the next step is to secure legal protection to prevent unauthorized use by competitors or other third parties. Trademarks, which protect symbols, names, and slogans used to distinguish goods or services, can be registered through the U.S. Patent and Trademark Office (USPTO). This registration provides nationwide protection and deters others from using a similar mark that could cause confusion. Copyrights, on the other hand, automatically protect original works of authorship such as books, articles, and even software code, from the moment they are created and fixed in a tangible form. However, formally registering copyrights can provide additional legal benefits, such as the ability to sue for statutory damages. For inventions, obtaining a patent can be a more complex process, involving a detailed disclosure of the invention and a review by the USPTO, but it grants an exclusive right to produce and sell the invention for a certain period.

Protecting your IP also involves vigilance against infringement, which can dilute your brand and eat into your profits. Keeping an eye on the market for potential infringements and conducting regular online searches can help you identify any unauthorized use of your IP. If you do find that your IP rights have been infringed upon, it's important to act swiftly. Initial steps might include sending a cease-and-desist letter to the infringer, which is often enough to stop the infringement. However, if the issue escalates, legal action may be necessary to enforce your rights. In such cases, consulting with an IP attorney can provide guidance on the best course of action, depending on the nature of the infringement and the impact on your business.

Another strategic aspect of managing your IP is considering the potential for licensing your intellectual property to others. Licensing can be a powerful way to generate revenue without the overhead associated with manufacturing and selling products yourself. For example, if your LLC owns a patent on a particular technology, licensing it to larger manufacturers could provide a steady stream of royalty payments. Similarly, if your business model doesn't directly utilize some of your copyrighted works, such as software or content, these can be licensed to other companies who can make use of them, bringing in additional revenue. Establishing clear, legally sound licensing agreements is crucial in these scenarios to ensure that your IP rights are respected and that the financial terms are favorable.

Navigating the complexities of intellectual property rights is essential for safeguarding the innovations and creative works that give your LLC its competitive edge. By identifying your IP, securing the appropriate legal protections, vigilantly monitoring for infringements, and exploring licensing opportunities, you can not only protect your business assets but also turn your intellectual property into a profitable cornerstone of your business strategy. These actions not only fortify your business against potential legal threats but also enhance its growth potential, positioning your LLC for long-term success in the marketplace.

RISKS: INSURANCE FOR LLCS

In the dynamic landscape of business, where unforeseen events can quickly escalate into financial losses, insurance stands as a crucial safeguard. For LLCs, selecting the right insurance policies is not merely an optional safety measure but a strategic foundation that protects both the company's assets and its operational future. Understanding the types of insurance that are pertinent to your business, assessing your specific needs, comparing offerings from various providers, and ensuring your coverage evolves with your business are all integral steps in fortifying your LLC against potential risks.

The portfolio of insurance for an LLC can be diverse, each type serving a specific purpose. *Liability insurance*, for example, is fundamental for nearly all businesses, providing protection against claims resulting from injuries and damage to people or property. *General liability insurance* covers common risks, including customer injuries at your place of business or damages caused by your employees. *Professional liability insurance*, also known as *errors and omissions insurance*, is crucial for businesses that provide services to clients, offering protection against claims of malpractice and negligence. For LLCs that own or lease physical spaces, *property insurance* is essential as it covers the business against losses due to fire, storms, theft, and other incidents that could damage business premises or equipment. Additionally, if your business involves manufacturing or using specialized equipment, you might consider *product liability insurance* to protect against claims of product-related injuries or damage.

Evaluating your LLC's specific insurance needs involves a careful analysis of your business activities, the assets you need to protect, and the risks inherent in your industry. Start by conducting a risk assessment to identify all potential vulnerabilities within your operations. Consider factors such as the nature of your products or services, the size of your operations, the number of employees, and your business location. For instance, if your LLC operates in a field with high legal exposure, such as healthcare or financial services, the importance of professional liability insurance increases significantly. Similarly, if you are based in an area prone to natural disasters, ensuring comprehensive property insurance should be a priority. Understanding these nuances will guide you in selecting insurance policies that provide adequate coverage for the specific risks your business faces.

Comparing insurance providers is a critical step in securing the best coverage for your LLC. Look beyond just the costs and examine the specifics of coverage options, the reputation of the insurer, their customer service quality, and the ease of filing claims. Utilize online comparison tools that allow you to view side-by-side specifics of policies from different insurers. Reading reviews and testimonials from other business owners can provide insights into the reliability and responsiveness of the insurance companies. Don't hesitate to reach out to insurance agents with your questions; a trustworthy provider will be transparent and helpful, willing to tailor their policies to suit your business's unique needs.

Regularly reviewing your insurance coverage ensures that it remains aligned with your LLC's current situation and future growth. As your business evolves, so do your liabilities and assets, which can necessitate changes in your insurance policies. Annual reviews of your coverage can reveal if there are gaps that need filling or if there are areas where you might now be over-insured. These reviews are also the opportune time to reassess your business's valuation and update it in your policies, ensuring that any new equipment, products, or expansions are adequately covered. This proactive approach not only adjusts to your changing business landscape but also optimizes your insurance expenditures, ensuring that your premiums are invested in necessary and sufficient coverage.

Navigating the complexities of insurance may seem daunting, but understanding and implementing these strategic steps transform insurance from a statutory obligation into a pivotal component of your business strategy. This approach not only protects your LLC from unexpected financial hardships but also builds a resilient foundation that supports your business's stability and growth. As you progress in your entrepreneurial endeavors, let this robust insurance strategy be the safety net that allows your business the freedom to innovate and expand with confidence.

HANDLING LEGAL DISPUTES AND LITIGATION

Legal disputes and litigation are a scenarios most business owners hope to avoid. Yet, understanding how to effectively manage and, more importantly, prevent these disputes is crucial for maintaining the smooth operation of your LLC. Disputes can arise in various aspects of business operations, from disagreements with partners or customers to employment issues with staff. Implementing proactive strategies to avoid these conflicts not only minimizes the risk of costly legal battles but also fosters a more harmonious business environment.

One effective strategy for avoiding legal disputes involves clear and thorough communication and documentation from the outset of any business relationship or agreement. For instance, when engaging with new partners or contractors, ensuring that all agreements are detailed and legally binding can prevent misinterpretations that might lead to disputes. Similarly, having comprehensive employment contracts and employee handbooks that clearly outline job duties, company policies, and behavioral expectations can mitigate potential misunderstandings with staff. Additionally, maintaining open lines of communication with partners, customers, and employees can help in addressing grievances before they escalate into more significant issues. Regular meetings and feedback sessions can be invaluable in this respect, providing a platform for concerns to be expressed and addressed promptly.

In situations where disputes do arise, resorting to litigation might not always be the best initial response. *Alternative dispute resolution (ADR)* methods such as mediation and arbitration can often provide a more cost-effective and less adversarial solution. We'll talk more about it in Chapter 7.

Knowing when to seek legal counsel is another critical aspect of managing disputes. While small disagreements might be resolved internally or through ADR methods, there are instances where legal advice is essential. Situations involving complex legal issues, significant amounts of money, or severe risks to your business's integrity should prompt you to consult with a lawyer. An experienced attorney can offer guidance on the legality of the issues at hand, represent your interests in negotiations or ADR processes, and prepare for litigation if it becomes necessary. Building a relationship with a legal advisor familiar with your business can also help you receive more tailored advice quickly when disputes arise.

Navigating the litigation process, if it comes to that, requires a strategic understanding of the legal steps involved. Litigation typically begins with the filing of a complaint by one party against another, outlining the nature of the dispute and the remedy sought. The other party then has the opportunity to file an answer, responding to the allegations put forth. This is followed by the discovery phase, where both sides exchange relevant information and evidence. Pretrial motions can resolve or narrow down the issues before heading to trial, where each side presents their case for a judge or jury to make a final decision. Throughout this process, having skilled legal representation is crucial as they can handle the intricacies of the case, from filing the right documents within deadlines to representing your interests in court. Additionally, understanding the potential costs, time commitments, and possible outcomes of litigation can help you make more informed decisions about pursuing or settling legal disputes.

By implementing clear communication practices, utilizing ADR methods effectively, knowing when to seek legal advice, and understanding the litigation process, you can manage and mitigate the risks associated with legal disputes in your LLC. These strategies not only protect your business legally and financially but also contribute to a more stable and harmonious business environment, allowing you to focus on growth and success.

UPDATING YOUR LLC OPERATING AGREEMENT

The operating agreement of your LLC serves as the foundational document that outlines the governance and operational guidelines of your business. It is a dynamic document, meant to evolve alongside your business as changes occur. The reasons to update an LLC's operating agreement are varied but pivotally important. They often involve adapting to changes in management structures, shifts in ownership, or expansions in the business's scope. For instance, if your LLC brings on new members or one of the original members exits, updating the operating agreement ensures that everyone's rights and responsibilities are clearly defined and agreed upon. Similarly, changes in state laws concerning LLCs might necessitate amendments to stay compliant and protect the business and its members.

Updating your operating agreement should be approached with careful consideration and a structured process. Typically, the agreement itself outlines the procedures for making amendments, which often require a certain percentage of member approval before changes can be enacted. This democratic approach ensures that all members have a voice in the evolution of the company. The process usually begins with a proposal for amendments, discussion among members, and a vote. If the necessary majority approves the amendment, the changes are documented and officially integrated into the operating agreement. It's crucial to record these amendments properly, not just in the meeting minutes but also by revising the official operating agreement document. This might involve drafting new sections or revising existing ones, then having all members sign the updated document to affirm their consent.

Common reasons for amendments often reflect the dynamic nature of business. Changes in management, for example, can trigger updates to clarify the roles and responsibilities of new or departing managers. Ownership changes, another typical catalyst for amendments, require adjustments to reflect the new structure of ownership and the distribution of profits and losses. This could mean updating the capital accounts of members or altering how decisions are made and approved within the LLC. Expanding the scope of the business is also a frequent motivator for amendments. As your LLC grows, you might venture into new markets or develop new product lines that require changes in how the business is run. The operating agreement needs to reflect these changes to provide clear guidelines on the management of new business activities.

Given the legal implications of these amendments, seeking legal assistance is highly advisable to ensure the updated operating agreement complies with current laws and remains enforceable. A legal professional specializing in business or corporate law can provide invaluable guidance on the necessary legal frameworks and help draft amendments that protect the interests of all members while promoting the growth and sustainability of the business. This legal oversight helps prevent potential disputes among members by ensuring that all amendments are clear, fair, and legally sound.

In essence, the operating agreement of your LLC is not just a static document but a living framework that should adapt to the evolving ramifications of your business and legal environments. By understanding when and why updates are needed, following a structured process for amendments, and seeking appropriate legal advice, you can ensure that your LLC's operating agreement continues to serve as a strong, relevant foundation for your business operations.

SUCCESSION PLANNING: PREPARING YOUR LLC FOR THE FUTURE

Succession planning is not merely a contingency plan; it is a proactive strategy that ensures your business can continue to thrive, even in your absence or that of other key members. It's about preparing your business today for the uncertainties of tomorrow. This preparation not only secures a smooth transition when changes in leadership or ownership occur but also enhances the confidence of employees, investors, and stakeholders.

Creating an effective succession plan requires a comprehensive approach. Begin by identifying key roles within your LLC, including your own, and assess the impact of these roles on your business operations. The next step involves identifying potential successors for these roles. These can be current employees who have shown the capability and interest to take on more responsibilities, or external candidates if internal talent does not align with future needs. Once potential successors are identified, the plan should outline the process and timeline for transitioning each key role. This includes detailing any interim positions that may act as stepping stones to prepare successors for their eventual roles.

Training and development play a pivotal role in equipping these chosen successors with the necessary skills and knowledge to lead your LLC effectively. This might involve targeted training programs, mentorship arrangements, and gradual involvement in decision-making processes to provide them with a deeper understanding of the business and its operations. Ensuring that this training aligns with the future direction and strategy of your business is crucial, as it prepares the new leaders not just to maintain the business but to drive it forward according to the established vision and goals.

Legal and financial considerations are also integral to a robust succession plan. From a legal perspective, changes in ownership or management may require updates to your LLC's operating agreement, particularly in terms of ownership shares and voting rights. It's advisable to consult with a legal professional to ensure that all modifications comply with existing laws and reflect the agreed terms among all parties involved. On the financial side, consider the tax implications of transferring ownership stakes, especially if the succession plan includes selling shares of the business. Proper financial planning can help mitigate potential tax burdens, making the transition smoother and financially viable for all parties. Furthermore, if the succession plan is triggered by retirement, disability, or death, life insurance policies or buy-sell agreements funded through insurance proceeds can provide the necessary funds to facilitate a buyout, ensuring the business has the financial means to execute the succession plan without major disruptions.

In essence, effective succession planning secures the legacy of your LLC beyond the tenure of its current leaders. It ensures that the business you have built is resilient enough to withstand transitions in leadership and ownership, preserving its operational integrity and strategic direction. By carefully selecting and preparing successors, and addressing the legal and financial aspects of these transitions, you create a roadmap that not only guides your LLC through future changes but also strengthens its foundation for continued growth and success.

As we conclude this chapter, remember that the strategies discussed here are designed to equip you with the knowledge and tools necessary to navigate the complexities of legal compliance and risk management effectively. These elements are crucial not only for safeguarding your business's present operations but also for securing its future through thoughtful succession planning. In the next chapter, we will explore strategies for expanding and scaling your LLC, ensuring that your business is not just prepared for the future but also poised for growth and success.

EXPANDING AND SCALING YOUR LLC

*A*s your LLC grows from its initial phases into a more established entity, you face new challenges and opportunities that demand innovative strategies and thoughtful planning. This chapter delves into the crucial aspects of expanding and scaling your business, focusing on identifying growth opportunities, diversifying your offerings, adopting innovative marketing strategies, and enhancing customer retention. Each of these areas represents a pivotal step towards not just enlarging your business footprint, but also solidifying its market position in a sustainable manner.

GROWTH STRATEGIES FOR SMALL LLCS: IDENTIFYING GROWTH OPPORTUNITIES

At the heart of any business expansion is the ability to spot and seize growth opportunities. For small LLCs, this often means looking beyond the obvious and finding niches or underserved markets. Start by analyzing your current business data—sales trends, customer feedback, and operational performance all offer insights into potential areas for expansion. For instance, if certain products or services consistently outperform others, it might indicate a market preference that you can capitalize on more aggressively.

Additionally, staying attuned to industry trends and shifts can reveal opportunities. This might involve adopting new technologies, tapping into emerging markets, or even anticipating regulatory changes that could affect your industry. Engaging with industry news, attending conferences, and participating in professional networks can provide you with valuable foresight. Remember, the goal is not just to keep up with your competitors but to anticipate the curve and be ready to act when opportunities arise.

Diversification

Diversifying your business can mitigate risks and increase your growth potential. This strategy involves expanding your product lines, exploring new services, or entering different markets. For example, if your LLC is in the manufacturing sector, diversification might mean offering customization options for your products, which could tap into a new customer segment. Alternatively, if you're providing a service, consider whether there are adjacent services that your existing customer base would find valuable.

Diversification also means thinking about geographic expansion. Is there a demand for your products or services in other regions or even internationally? Before making such moves, ensure you conduct thorough market research to understand the new market's dynamics and customer preferences, which might differ significantly from your current base.

Innovative Marketing

In today's digital age, traditional marketing strategies might not suffice to cut through the noise. Innovative marketing strategies such as influencer partnerships, experiential marketing, and targeted social media campaigns can significantly boost your business's visibility and engagement. For instance, collaborating with influencers who resonate with your brand can provide access to a broader audience that trusts the influencer's recommendations.

Experiential marketing, creating unique, real-world experiences that immerse customers in your brand, can also create lasting impressions and build strong emotional connections with your products. This could be as simple as in-store events or as elaborate as interactive pop-up installations in high-traffic areas. The key is to create experiences that not only reflect your brand's values but also actively involve the customer, making the interaction memorable and sharable.

Customer Retention

While attracting new customers is crucial, retaining existing ones offers more value over time. Implementing effective customer retention strategies can ensure sustained revenue growth and build a loyal customer base that champions your brand. Start by understanding your customers' needs and expectations through regular feedback and engagement. Tools like customer surveys, feedback forms, and direct interactions can provide insights into what your customers value most and any areas needing improvement.

Personalization of services or products can also enhance customer retention. Using data analytics to tailor your offerings or communications to fit individual customer preferences shows that you value their business and understand their needs. Moreover, implementing loyalty programs, offering exclusive discounts, or providing exceptional customer service can all contribute to high customer satisfaction and repeat business.

Visual Element: Customer Feedback Form

A well-designed customer feedback form can be a beneficial tool for understanding your customers' satisfaction and areas for improvement. Use this form after a purchase or interaction with your customer to gather insights that can guide your customer retention strategies. Ensure the form is concise, focused, and easy to fill out, whether it's in a digital format or on paper. Include questions that measure satisfaction with your products or services, ask for suggestions for improvement, and inquire about the likelihood of recommending your business to others.

By integrating these strategies into your business operations, you are not just expanding your LLC but are also building a resilient, adaptable, and customer-focused enterprise that stands ready to meet future challenges and seize new opportunities. As you continue to explore the diverse facets of business expansion in the following sections, keep in mind that each strategy should align with your overall business goals and values, ensuring that growth is not just achieved but sustained over the long term.

FINANCING OPTIONS FOR EXPANDING YOUR LLC

Self-Financing

When considering expanding your LLC, self-financing can be a compelling option. This method involves using your own savings or reinvesting profits back into the business. One of the key advantages of self-financing is control. You maintain complete control over your business without the need to consult external funders or adjust your business plan to meet their criteria. Additionally, by not seeking external funding, you avoid diluting your ownership and potentially losing a portion of your future profits to investors. Reinvesting profits also demonstrates to stakeholders that you have skin in the game, which can be crucial for building trust and credibility.

However, self-financing is not without risks. It can significantly drain your personal savings and reduce the financial safety net you might otherwise depend on. Moreover, by reinvesting profits, you may limit your business's ability to cope with unforeseen expenses. It's crucial to assess your financial landscape thoroughly, ensuring that this approach doesn't stretch your personal or business finances too thin. A balanced viewpoint considering both the potential for growth and the risks of limited liquidity will guide you in making a prudent decision regarding self-financing.

Loans and Credit

Access to capital is often a necessity for expanding businesses, and securing loans or lines of credit is a common approach. Traditional bank loans might be the first option that comes to mind. These are typically installment loans where you receive a lump sum and agree to pay it back, plus interest, over a predetermined period. To secure such a loan, you'll need to demonstrate your business's profitability and ability to repay the loan, which usually involves presenting detailed financial records and a solid business plan.

Alternatively, lines of credit offer more flexibility. Rather than receiving a lump sum, a line of credit provides access to funds up to a certain limit that you can draw upon as needed. This can be particularly useful for managing cash flow fluctuations or unexpected expenses. For small businesses looking to expand, the U.S. Small Business Administration (SBA) offers a variety of loan programs that are designed to meet the needs of different business scenarios. SBA loans are generally more accessible to startups and small businesses that might not qualify for traditional bank loans due to a lack of credit history or collateral. The terms of SBA loans are often favorable, with lower interest rates and longer repayment terms, which can ease the financial pressure on your expanding business.

Investors

Seeking external investors, including angel investors and venture capitalists, is another route to finance expansion. *Angel investors* are individuals who provide capital for startups businesses or small businesses in exchange for equity in your business (ownership) or a convertible debt into future shares. They are often found among an entrepreneur's family and friends or can be professional who not only bring funds but also their expertise and networks. *Venture capitalists*, on the other hand, are firms that manage pooled funds from many investors to invest in startups and small businesses that have high growth potential.

While both types of investors can provide significant capital, they usually seek businesses with the potential for a high return on investment. Attracting these investors requires a compelling business plan, a clear path to significant growth, and a persuasive pitch. It's important to consider the implications of giving up equity and the potential for pressure to rapidly scale the business. The relationships with these investors should be nurtured, as their expertise and networks can be as valuable as their capital.

Crowdfunding

Crowdfunding has emerged as a modern financing solution, particularly attractive for businesses that engage directly with consumers. Platforms like *Kickstarter*, *Indiegogo*, and *GoFundMe* allow you to present your business idea or expansion plan to the public, soliciting small investments from a large number of people. This method not only raises funds but can also validate your product and build a community of supporters.

Successful crowdfunding campaigns require a compelling story and effective promotion, often through social media and other digital marketing channels. The rewards offered to backers, such as early access to products or exclusive perks, must be carefully considered to encourage contributions while maintaining profitability. It's also essential to understand the specific rules and fees associated with the crowdfunding platform you choose, as well as the need to fulfill any commitments made to backers to maintain trust and credibility.

Each of these financing options offers different advantages and challenges, and the right choice depends on your specific business needs, your financial situation, and your long-term business goals. As you consider these options, think about how they align with your plans for expansion and the overall vision for your LLC.

ENTERING NEW MARKETS TO EXPAND YOUR BUSINESS

Market Research

When you're considering taking your LLC into new geographical territories, the foundational step is conducting exhaustive market research. This process is essential not only to understand the potential of the new market but also to tailor your strategies effectively. Start by identifying and segmenting your target demographics. Who are they? What are their purchasing behaviors, preferences, and needs? Tools such as surveys, focus groups, and market analysis reports can provide deep insights into these questions. Also, analyze your competitors in the market. Who are the major players? What are their strengths and weaknesses? How does your business compare, and what unique value can you offer that they don't?

Furthermore, consider the economic and socio-political environment of the market. Factors such as economic stability, currency exchange rates, and local laws can significantly affect your business operations. For instance, a region experiencing economic growth and stability might present a favorable environment for introducing luxury products. On the other hand, markets with stringent trade laws or high tariffs might require a different approach or reconsideration altogether. Utilizing data analytics can also provide predictive insights into market trends, helping you to make data-driven decisions. This thorough understanding will not only minimize the risks associated with entering a new market but also enhance your chances of successfully establishing your brand.

Localization Strategies

Once you have a grasp of the new market through comprehensive research, the next crucial step is localization. This means adapting your products and marketing strategies to align with local tastes, cultural norms, and languages. For instance, if your product labels are originally in English and you're entering a market where another language is predominant, translating your materials shows respect for the local culture and increases your product's appeal. Similarly, consider the cultural nuances that might affect the perception of your product. In some cultures, certain colors or numbers might have significant meanings that can impact product packaging or marketing materials.

Localization also extends to marketing strategies. Digital marketing tactics that work in one region may not be as effective in another due to differences in digital platform popularity or marketing regulations. For example, while Facebook and Instagram might be the go-to platforms in one country, another might rely more heavily on platforms like Twitter or unique local platforms. Tailoring your digital campaigns to fit these preferences increases your visibility and engagement with potential customers. Additionally, localized SEO strategies can help your business become more visible in local search engine results, which is crucial for driving traffic to your site and increasing local sales.

Pilot Programs

Before rolling out your business on a full scale, consider starting with a pilot program. This limited-scale launch allows you to test your product or service in the market without the full investment and risk associated with a complete launch. Choose a representative sample of your target market to test aspects like product appeal, pricing strategies, and promotional tactics. The feedback and data gathered from this pilot program can be invaluable. It allows you to tweak your product, adjust your marketing strategies, and even streamline your supply chain as needed before a full-scale launch.

This approach not only minimizes financial risks but also provides a practical insight into the market's response to your offerings. It acts as a final verification of all the adaptations and strategies you've planned based on your market research and localization efforts. If the pilot program is successful, you can proceed with confidence, knowing that your business is more likely to resonate with the local market. If not, it provides a crucial checkpoint to reevaluate and adjust your strategies without significant losses.

Entering new markets is a bold step that can significantly enhance the growth and profitability of your LLC if done correctly. By carefully researching the market, localizing your approach, adhering to regulatory requirements, and testing the waters with a pilot program, you lay a strong foundation for successful market entry. These steps, taken meticulously and thoughtfully, prepare your LLC not just to enter new markets but to thrive in them, driving your business to new heights of success.

STRATEGIC PARTNERSHIPS AND COLLABORATIONS

Forming strategic partnerships and collaborations can significantly amplify the growth and outreach of your LLC. These alliances can provide access to new markets, technologies, and expertise that might otherwise be out of reach. The benefits of such partnerships are manifold. For starters, they can help reduce costs by sharing resources such as marketing expenses, technology platforms, and even staff. They also offer an opportunity to enhance your business offering by combining strengths, which can lead to innovative solutions and services that better meet customer needs. Furthermore, strategic partnerships can increase your bargaining power and provide a competitive edge by aligning with other entities that complement or enhance your business capabilities.

EXPANDING AND SCALING YOUR LLC

When considering potential partners, the alignment of goals is crucial. Look for companies or entrepreneurs who not only share similar objectives but also have a compatible business culture. This alignment ensures that both parties are working towards a common end, making it easier to overcome challenges and disagreements that may arise. To find these partners, start by networking within your industry through trade shows, conferences, and seminars. Online platforms like LinkedIn can also be instrumental in identifying and connecting with potential partners. Additionally, consider leveraging existing relationships with vendors, clients, and even competitors, as these entities already understand your business and may be open to deeper collaborations.

Once you identify potential partners, the negotiation of terms becomes paramount. These discussions should aim to create a win-win situation where the value is evident to both parties. Key elements of partnership agreements include clear roles and responsibilities, financial contributions, profit-sharing models, and conflict resolution mechanisms. It is often beneficial to involve legal counsel in these discussions to ensure that the agreements are not only fair but also legally sound. Transparent communication from the outset about expectations and the strategic goals of the partnership can prevent misunderstandings and set the stage for a successful collaboration.

Managing these partnerships requires ongoing effort. Regular meetings and open lines of communication are essential to ensure that all parties remain aligned with the partnership's goals. It's also important to establish key performance indicators (KPIs) that help measure the success of the collaboration. These metrics can include financial targets, customer satisfaction rates, or other relevant benchmarks that provide insight into the partnership's effectiveness. Celebrating shared successes and learning from setbacks can strengthen the partnership and encourage continued collaboration. Additionally, being adaptable and open to adjusting the terms of the partnership in response to changing market conditions or strategic shifts in the business can help sustain the relationship over the long term.

Strategic partnerships and collaborations, when managed well, not only fuel business growth but also enhance innovation and market adaptability. By carefully selecting the right partners, crafting mutually beneficial agreements, and managing the relationship effectively, your LLC can leverage these alliances to achieve more than it could alone. As you continue to explore and develop these strategic relationships, remember that the strength of a partnership lies not just in the strategic alignment but also in the commitment to mutual success and the ongoing effort to maintain a healthy, productive relationship.

SCALING OPERATIONS: WHEN TO AUTOMATE AND OUTSOURCE

As your LLC grows, the strategies and processes that once served you well may start to become bottlenecks, hindering further growth and efficiency. Recognizing when and how to scale your operations is crucial to sustaining your business's expansion while maintaining or improving quality and efficiency. The initial step in this process is to assess your current operations critically to identify areas where scalability is limited. This involves a thorough analysis of your workflow, identifying processes that are time-consuming, prone to errors, or disproportionately costly. Tools like workflow diagrams can help visually map out your processes, making it easier to pinpoint where delays or bottle-necks occur.

For instance, if you find that a significant amount of time is spent on data entry tasks that could be automated, this is an area ripe for improvement. Similarly, if customer service inquiries are increasing as your customer base grows, but your response times are lagging, this could indicate a need for scaling your customer service capabilities. It's also important to consider the scalability of your production capacity if you're manufacturing products. Are your current facilities capable of increasing production if demand rises? If not, what changes need to be made? This comprehensive assessment not only highlights current inefficiencies but also sets the stage for integrating solutions that can enhance scalability.

Automation solutions can play a pivotal role in streamlining oper-ations and increasing efficiency as your business scales. In today's tech-driven environment, automation tools are available for a wide range of business functions, from accounting and customer relationship management (CRM) to marketing and production. For example, CRM software can automate customer interaction tracking, helping you manage an increasing number of customer relationships without compromising the quality of service. Auto-mated marketing tools can handle tasks like email campaigns and social media posts, ensuring consistent marketing efforts as your business grows. On the production side, advanced manufacturing technologies like CNC machines or robotic assembly lines can dramatically increase production rates and precision.

Implementing these automation solutions typically involves an upfront investment in technology and training, but the long-term benefits can be substantial. Reduced labor costs, increased production speeds, error reduction, and freeing up human resources to focus on more strategic tasks are just a few of the advantages. However, choosing the right technologies and implementing them effectively requires a careful approach. Evaluate potential tools based on their compatibility with your existing systems, ease of use, and scalability. It's often wise to start with one or two processes to automate, measure the outcomes, and then gradually expand to other areas of your business.

Outsourcing is another strategy that can facilitate scaling, especially when certain functions of your business require specialized skills or equipment that are not core to your business operations. For example, outsourcing logistics to a third-party logistics provider can free you from the complexities of warehousing and shipping, allowing you to focus on product development and marketing. Similarly, outsourcing tasks like payroll processing or IT management can ensure that these critical functions are handled by experts, reducing your risk and overhead costs.

When considering outsourcing, it's important to carefully select your partners. Look for providers who not only offer the expertise you need but also share your commitment to quality and customer service. Establishing clear communication channels and performance metrics from the outset can help ensure that the outsourcing relationship supports your business goals. Remember, while outsourcing can offer significant benefits, it's crucial to maintain oversight to ensure that the quality of work meets your standards and that the outsourcing arrangement remains aligned with your business objectives.

Managing the challenges that come with rapid growth involves more than just expanding your capacity; it also requires maintaining the quality of your products or services and preserving your company culture. As your business grows, maintaining a focus on quality assurance processes is essential. Regularly review and adjust these processes as needed to accommodate increased production or service loads. Additionally, as more people join your organization, embedding your company culture through training programs, regular communications, and company events can help ensure that your values and standards permeate throughout the organization.

Scaling your operations effectively demands a strategic approach to automation, outsourcing, and management practices. By thoughtfully integrating these elements into your growth strategy, you can ensure that your LLC not only grows in size but also in capability, efficiency, and market strength.

PREPARING FOR ACQUISITION: POSITIONING YOUR LLC

When contemplating the future trajectory of your LLC, acquisition might emerge as a strategic avenue, either as a method to expand your business's reach or as a graceful exit strategy. The allure of acquisition lies in its potential to offer immediate financial reward, access to new markets, and enhanced operational capabilities through synergies with the acquiring entity. Understanding why and how to prepare your business for this complex process is crucial for achieving a successful transition.

The decision to position your LLC for acquisition typically stems from various motivations. For some, it's a planned exit strategy that aims to maximize the return on the years spent building the business. For others, it might be a strategic move to align with a larger entity that can propel the business to heights that would be challenging to achieve independently. In both scenarios, the preparation phase is pivotal. This involves not just sprucing up your financial statements, but also ensuring that all aspects of your business—from operational efficiency to customer relations —are functioning optimally to attract potential acquirers.

Valuing your business accurately is the cornerstone of preparing for an acquisition. The valuation process provides a quantifiable measure of your business's worth, which is crucial for negotiating with potential buyers. Common methods for valuing an LLC include the *asset-based approach*, which totals the values of all assets and subtracts liabilities; the *income approach*, which forecasts future cash flows and discounts them to present value; and the *market approach*, which involves comparing your business to similar businesses that have recently been sold. Engaging with a professional appraiser can lend credibility to your valuation and help you understand the factors that drive your business's value, from recurring revenue streams and market position to intellectual property and customer base.

Making your business more attractive to potential acquirers involves more than just a robust bottom line. It includes ensuring that your business operations are streamlined and that key processes are well-documented, which can significantly ease the transition post-acquisition. Additionally, diversifying your customer base and securing long-term customer contracts can make your business a more lucrative and secure investment. Maintaining a strong, clear brand identity and a solid online presence can also add to your attractiveness, as these elements indicate a healthy, forward-thinking business. It's also wise to resolve any outstanding legal issues and ensure compliance with relevant industry regulations to make your business a less risky and more appealing proposition.

Navigating the acquisition process itself involves several stages, starting with due diligence, where potential acquirers evaluate your business in detail to confirm its financial health and operational viability. This stage is critical and can influence the final offer from the acquirer. It's followed by negotiation, where the terms of the acquisition, including the purchase price, payment methods, and post-acquisition responsibilities, are agreed upon. Legal documentation then formalizes these terms. Throughout this process, having experienced advisors, such as a lawyer who specializes in mergers and acquisitions and a trusted financial advisor, is priceless. They can guide you through negotiations, help you understand the legal implications of the deal, and ensure that your interests are well-protected.

Preparing for an acquisition is a multifaceted process that requires thoughtful planning and execution. By understanding the motivations for acquisition, accurately valuing your business, making your operation attractive to buyers, and skillfully navigating the acquisition process, you position your LLC not just for a successful sale but also for a prosperous future under new ownership. This strategic approach not only enhances your negotiating power but also ensures that the legacy of your business is preserved and its potential fully realized.

As we close this section on preparing your LLC for acquisition, reflect on how this strategic move could serve as either a pinnacle achievement of your entrepreneurial efforts or as a stepping stone to further business adventures. The insights and strategies discussed here pave the way for you to approach potential acquisitions with confidence and foresight. Up next, we will explore how to protect your LLC through advanced asset protection strategies, ensuring that as your business grows and potentially transitions into new hands, it remains secure and robust against any legal or financial challenges that may arise.

PROTECTING YOUR LLC

$\mathcal{I}$n the dynamic world of business, where uncertainty is the only certainty, protecting your LLC goes beyond merely managing daily operations effectively. It involves proactive strategies to safeguard your assets against potential legal threats and financial pitfalls. This chapter unveils advanced asset protection strategies tailor-made for you, the astute entrepreneur, who understands that the true strength of a business lies not only in its ability to generate profit but also in its capacity to shield its resources from unforeseen adversities.

ADVANCED ASSET PROTECTION STRATEGIES FOR LLC OWNERS

Layering Legal Entities

One of the most effective strategies to protect your business assets is through the strategic use of multiple legal entities. By structuring your business to include holding companies, you can create a robust defensive mechanism against potential lawsuits and creditors. Here's how it works: a holding company is an entity that doesn't engage in any operational business activities but owns assets, such as intellectual property, real estate, or shares in other companies. This separation of asset ownership from the business activities carried out by your operating LLC acts as a barrier, safeguarding your valuable assets from any claims against the operating company.

For instance, imagine your LLC is sued for breach of contract. If your valuable assets like property or proprietary software are held by a separate holding company, these assets are typically not reachable by the creditors of the operating LLC. This structure not only minimizes your risk but also provides you an orderly way to manage different assets under a clear, organized framework. Setting up such a structure requires careful planning and adherence to legal protocols to ensure compliance and effectiveness, making consultation with a legal expert in business structuring indispensable.

International Asset Protection Trusts

For entrepreneurs looking to fortify their asset protection strategy, *International Asset Protection Trusts (IAPTs)* offer a formidable shield. These trusts are set up under the jurisdictions of countries with favorable asset protection laws, such as the Cook Islands or Belize, which do not recognize foreign judgments and have strong confidentiality features. By transferring the ownership of your assets to an IAPT, you place them beyond the easy reach of domestic creditors and legal actions.

However, the use of IAPTs involves navigating complex international laws and significant ethical considerations. It's crucial to understand that these trusts should be set up not as a means to evade lawful responsibilities or debts but as a preventive measure to protect against unjust or frivolous claims. Transparency with creditors and compliance with all legal requirements are key to ethically managing an IAPT. Given the complexities, engaging with an attorney who specializes in international trust law is essential to ensure that your IAPT is established correctly and operates within the legal frameworks.

Equity Stripping

Another strategic method to protect your assets is equity stripping, which can be particularly useful if you own real estate or other substantial tangible assets. Equity stripping involves decreasing the equity value of an asset on paper, making it less attractive to creditors. One common way to achieve this is through home equity lines of credit (HELOC). By placing a line of credit against the property, you essentially encumber it with debt, thus reducing its net equity value. In the event of a legal judgment against you, the reduced equity makes the asset less appealing for creditors to pursue.

It's important to proceed with caution when implementing equity stripping, as it involves taking on actual debt, which can impact your financial health if not managed wisely. Furthermore, this strategy should be part of a broader asset protection plan, complemented by other methods to ensure comprehensive protection. Consulting with financial and legal advisors to understand the implications and establish a balanced approach to equity stripping is advisable.

Insurance Solutions

Beyond traditional business liability insurance, there are specialized insurance products designed to offer additional layers of asset protection. For example, *umbrella insurance policies* provide extra coverage beyond the limits of your standard liability policies, covering claims that may exceed other insurance policies. Another example is *errors and omissions insurance*, which is particularly beneficial for businesses that provide professional services, as it protects against claims of negligence or failure to perform professional duties.

Investing in the right insurance coverage is akin to building a safety net that catches unforeseen liabilities potentially threatening your business. Assessing your business's specific risks and discussing them with an insurance broker can help you determine the appropriate types and levels of coverage, ensuring that your LLC is well-protected against various vulnerabilities.

Protecting your LLC is a multifaceted endeavor that requires a strategic approach and careful planning. By employing advanced asset protection strategies such as layering legal entities, setting up international trusts, implementing equity stripping, and securing specialized insurance products, you fortify your business against potential threats. This proactive stance not only safeguards your assets but also ensures the long-term stability and integrity of your business, allowing you to pursue your entrepreneurial goals with greater confidence and security.

PRIVACY PROTECTION AND DATA SECURITY FOR YOUR LLC

In today's digital age, safeguarding the private data of your business and your clients is not just a strategic advantage—it is a fundamental necessity. Understanding and adhering to data privacy laws such as the General Data Protection Regulation (GDPR) and the California Consumer Privacy Act (CCPA) can significantly impact how your LLC operates, especially if your business activities span across different regions. Both GDPR and CCPA dictate stringent requirements for data handling and grant significant rights to individuals regarding their personal data, irrespective of whether your business physically operates within Europe or California. Non-compliance can result in hefty fines and a tarnished reputation, which could deter potential clients and partners.

For instance, *GDPR* affects any business that processes the personal data of EU residents, emphasizing transparency, security, and accountability by data controllers and processors. Your LLC must ensure that personal data is gathered legally and under strict conditions, and those who collect and manage it are obliged to protect it from misuse and exploitation, as well as to respect the rights of data owners. On the other hand, *CCPA* provides California residents with the right to know about the personal data collected about them and whether their personal data is being sold or disclosed and to whom. They also have the right to say no to the sale of personal data. Implementing these laws into your LLC's operations requires a comprehensive data protection strategy that addresses these legal requirements.

Creating and implementing a robust data security plan is your next big step. It starts with understanding the specific types of data your business collects, where it comes from, how it is used, and who has access to it. This inventory forms the basis for developing policies that dictate how data should be handled and protected. Employee training is crucial in this plan. Your team should understand the importance of data security and be familiar with your security policies to ensure they handle data appropriately and recognize potential security threats. Regular training sessions can keep these practices top of mind. Additionally, establish protocols for responding to data breaches, including how to identify and report a breach, steps to contain it, and methods to assess and mitigate any damage. These response strategies not only help in managing the situation more effectively but also in maintaining trust with your clients by dealing with breaches transparently and efficiently.

Technology plays a pivotal role in protecting your digital assets and customer information. Encryption technologies are essential tools in your data security arsenal, helping protect data at rest and in transit. By encoding your data, encryption ensures that even if an unauthorized party accesses the data, they cannot interpret it. Consider implementing full-disk encryption on all your business devices; this ensures that all data stored on the device is encrypted automatically. Secure data storage solutions, such as cloud services that offer built-in encryption and robust security measures, can further safeguard your data.

Regular security audits and compliance checks are indispensable for ensuring that your data protection measures are effective and that your business remains compliant with applicable laws. These audits involve a thorough examination of your IT infrastructure, including databases, networks, and applications, to identify vulnerabilities that could be exploited by cyber threats. Conducting these audits regularly helps you stay ahead of potential security issues and fortify your defenses. Compliance checks should also be a routine part of your audit process, ensuring that your data handling practices continue to align with legal requirements. This proactive approach not only helps mitigate risks but also demonstrates to your clients and partners that your LLC is committed to maintaining high standards of data security and compliance.

By integrating these strategies into your business operations, you establish a framework that not only protects against data breaches and compliance issues but also builds a foundation of trust with your clients, enhancing your LLC's reputation and operational stability. As you move forward, remember that data security is not a one-time task but an ongoing process of improvement and adaptation to new challenges and regulations. This commitment to continuous enhancement of your data protection practices will serve as a cornerstone of your business's resilience and integrity in the digital landscape.

NAVIGATING BANKRUPTCY AND FINANCIAL DISTRESS

When facing financial challenges, understanding your options for bankruptcy and strategies for creditor negotiations can be critical for protecting your LLC and planning a path to recovery. Bankruptcy, although often seen as a last resort, can sometimes provide a structured way to address insolvency and offer a chance to rebuild. The U.S. Bankruptcy Code offers several chapters under which businesses, including LLCs, can file, primarily Chapter 7, Chapter 11, and Chapter 13, each serving different business needs and situations.

Chapter 7 bankruptcy, often referred to as liquidation bankruptcy, involves the dissolution of the business. The appointed trustee sells the company's assets to pay off creditors. This option is generally considered when the LLC has no viable future or significant assets that need to be preserved for operating the business. It's a way to gracefully exit the market, settle debts, and eliminate personal liability on business debts, provided proper corporate formalities have been observed to avoid personal guarantees on loans.

On the other hand, *Chapter 11 bankruptcy* is designed for reorganization rather than liquidation. This route is often favored by businesses that believe the company can be profitable again with a little time and restructuring. In Chapter 11, you can keep your business operational while renegotiating terms with creditors under the supervision of the bankruptcy court. This process allows you to restructure debts and potentially reduce obligations, giving your business a second chance to regain profitability under a revised business model.

Chapter 13 bankruptcy is less common for LLCs, as it's primarily designed for individuals, including sole proprietors. It allows for debt restructuring under a repayment plan that spans three to five years, enabling the debtor to keep their property and pay off debts over time. While it's not typically used for LLCs, understanding this option is still helpful, especially for sole proprietors operating their businesses as LLCs who might benefit from this personal bankruptcy protection impacting their business liabilities.

For LLCs considering bankruptcy, asset protection strategies play a crucial role in the process. Utilizing state exemptions where applicable can shield certain assets from liquidation in Chapter 7 or influence the restructuring plan in Chapter 11. Strategic transfers of assets prior to bankruptcy, not meant to defraud creditors but as part of legitimate estate planning or business operations, might also protect assets from being included in the bankruptcy estate. However, it's crucial these transfers are done with transparency and legal consultation to avoid allegations of fraudulent transfers designed to merely shield assets from creditors.

Negotiating with creditors is another critical strategy that can sometimes prevent the need for bankruptcy. When cash flow challenges arise, reaching out proactively to creditors to negotiate repayment terms can be beneficial. Techniques include requesting extended payment terms, reducing the interest rate, or even settling debts for a lump sum that is less than the full amount owed. Effective negotiation can preserve vital business relationships and provide your LLC the breathing room needed to restore financial stability. Demonstrating a clear plan for repayment and being open about your financial difficulties can foster cooperation from creditors, who generally prefer to receive some form of repayment rather than risk losing all in a bankruptcy proceeding.

Recovery and rebuilding post-bankruptcy are pivotal for entrepreneurs who have undergone the challenging process of bankruptcy. The focus should be on restoring creditworthiness and operational stability. This starts with adhering to the post-bankruptcy repayment plan and ensuring all obligations under the bankruptcy terms are met punctually. Rebuilding credit can also involve taking on new credit responsibly and making all payments on time to gradually restore lenders' trust. Additionally, analyzing the reasons that led to bankruptcy, whether inadequate cash flow management, insufficient demand for the product or service, or external economic factors, can provide valuable lessons. Implementing stronger financial controls, diversifying income streams, and maintaining a lean operational model can help prevent future financial distress, setting a stronger foundation for sustainable business operations moving forward.

LEGAL STRATEGIES FOR MINIMIZING LIABILITY

Contracts and Agreements

When you're navigating the complexities of running your LLC, one of the most powerful tools at your disposal is the strategic use of *contracts* and *agreements*. These legal documents, when crafted carefully, serve as the first line of defense in limiting liability and protecting your business interests. The inclusion of indemnity clauses and liability waivers in your contracts can significantly fortify this defense, providing clear terms that can shield your LLC from potential legal claims.

Indemnity clauses, for instance, are designed to allocate the risks associated with business operations. They work by specifying that if certain events occur, resulting in loss or damage, one party agrees to compensate the other. For example, if you're contracting with a supplier, an indemnity clause can require the supplier to compensate your LLC if their actions lead to product failure that causes you financial harm. Similarly, *liability waivers* are critical when your business activities could expose you to claims of damages from third parties. These waivers are particularly common in service agreements where customers agree to not hold your LLC liable for injuries or damages they might incur as a result of engaging with your services under normal circumstances.

Crafting these agreements requires a nuanced understanding of your business operations and potential risks. It's advisable to work closely with a legal professional who can help draft contracts that not only meet legal standards but also strategically mitigate potential liabilities. Moreover, ensuring that these contracts are reviewed regularly to align with new laws or changes in business operations can prevent loopholes that might leave your LLC vulnerable to claims.

Proactive Compliance Programs

Another cornerstone of minimizing liability for your LLC involves establishing proactive compliance programs. These programs serve as an operational blueprint that guides your team in adhering to legal statutes and industry regulations, thereby mitigating risks associated with regulatory violations. A robust compliance program typically includes a detailed risk assessment of your business operations, clear policies and procedures that address these risks, regular training for employees, and an effective monitoring system to ensure ongoing compliance.

Implementing such a program starts with understanding the specific regulations that impact your business. This might include federal and state laws related to consumer protection, employment, environmental standards, and more. By integrating these legal requirements into your everyday business processes and decision-making, you create a culture of compliance that permeates all levels of your organization. Regular training sessions help keep your team updated on their compliance responsibilities and the importance of their role in protecting the LLC. Additionally, setting up an internal reporting system for compliance issues encourages transparency and swift action to rectify problems before they escalate into costly legal challenges.

Dispute Resolution Mechanisms

Incorporating alternative dispute resolution (ADR) mechanisms such as arbitration clauses into your business dealings can provide a significant safeguard against the time, costs, and uncertainties associated with traditional litigation. Arbitration, in particular, offers a more private and potentially quicker way to resolve disputes. By including an arbitration clause in your contracts, both parties agree to resolve any disputes through arbitration rather than through court proceedings. This not only helps in maintaining business relationships by avoiding the adversarial nature of court disputes but also enhances control over the resolution process, as parties can choose knowledgeable arbitrators who specialize in the specific subject matter relevant to the dispute.

Implementing arbitration effectively requires careful drafting of arbitration clauses to ensure they are enforceable and tailored to your specific business needs. Considerations include defining the scope of disputes covered, the rules for selecting arbitrators, the arbitration process, and how the arbitrator's decisions will be enforced. Regular reviews of these clauses are crucial to adapt to changes in law and business operations, ensuring they continue to provide a reliable framework for dispute resolution.

Professional Liability Insurance

Finally, evaluating the need for professional liability insurance is crucial in rounding out your strategy to minimize liability. This type of insurance provides protection against claims of negligence or harm caused by mistakes or failure to perform. It's particularly important if your LLC provides professional services, such as consulting, medical advice, or legal services, where such claims could be financially devastating.

Determining the right coverage involves assessing the specific risks associated with your LLC's operations. Factors to consider include the nature of your services, the potential for significant financial loss by clients due to errors, and the overall risk environment of your industry. Consulting with an insurance broker who understands your industry can help tailor a policy that meets your specific needs, providing peace of mind and financial protection.

By integrating these legal strategies into your LLC's operations, you actively work to minimize potential liabilities, ensuring not just compliance and good governance, but also securing a more stable and confident path forward for your business endeavors.

HANDLING BUSINESS DIVORCE IN MULTI-MEMBER LLCS

When multiple partners come together to form an LLC, the synergy can drive the business to new heights. However, just as in any relationship, disagreements or changes in individual goals can lead to a situation commonly referred to as a 'business divorce'. Managing such a separation amicably and efficiently is crucial to maintaining the continuity of the business and protecting the interests of all parties involved. One of the first lines of defense in such scenarios is a well-drafted *buy-sell agreement*. This legal document functions as a prenuptial agreement for your business, detailing how a member's share of the business may be reassigned if they wish to leave or are forced to exit due to circumstances like death or incapacity.

A comprehensive buy-sell agreement addresses potential triggers for a business divorce and outlines the methodology for valuing the departing member's interest. This is critical because disputes over valuation can escalate, leading to prolonged legal battles that drain resources and distract from business operations. The agreement should specify whether the remaining members have the right to buy out the departing member and at what price. Methods for valuation can vary, but common approaches include using a formula specified in the agreement, agreeing to a third-party valuation, or a combination of both to ensure fairness and transparency.

When disagreements over valuation or other terms do arise, resorting to litigation can seem like a straightforward solution, but it's often time-consuming and costly. Instead, embedding mediation and arbitration clauses within the LLC operating agreement or the buy-sell agreement itself can provide a path to resolution that is typically quicker and less adversarial. Mediation involves a neutral third-party facilitator who helps both sides reach a voluntary agreement. It's a flexible process that allows for creative solutions that courts might not legally be able to impose. Arbitration, on the other hand, involves a third-party arbitrator who remains neutral and listens to both sides and makes a binding decision. Both methods have the advantage of being less formal than court proceedings, which can preserve personal relationships and the professional reputation of the business.

Another significant aspect of handling a business divorce is ensuring the continuity of the LLC once a member departs. This is where effective succession planning plays a crucial role. It involves more than just deciding who will take over responsibilities; it includes planning for the transfer of ownership interests to ensure the business continues operating smoothly without disruption. Succession planning should be thought of as an ongoing strategy, initiated from the early days of the business and revisited regularly as circumstances within the business and its environment evolve. This proactive approach not only prepares the LLC for potential departures but also positions it to seize opportunities, such as bringing in new talent or capital that can drive future growth.

Handling a business divorce in a multi-member LLC necessitates a blend of foresight, structured legal agreements, and strategies for dispute resolution. By establishing clear agreements and procedures from the outset, you can safeguard the business's operations and ensure its resilience through transitions, allowing the business to remain robust and focused on its long-term goals. This strategic preparation not only protects the interests of all members but also fortifies the business against the potential upheavals that personal disagreements or changes might bring. As you navigate these complex dynamics, remember that the strength of your LLC lies in its ability to adapt and manage transitions smoothly, preserving the legacy and the strategic vision upon which it was built.

THE ROLE OF LEGAL COUNSEL IN LLC MANAGEMENT

Having a seasoned attorney by your side isn't just helpful—it's a strategic necessity. Recognizing when to seek legal advice is crucial. Situations that typically require professional legal insight include drafting or reviewing contracts, handling disputes or litigation, managing intellectual property, undergoing mergers or acquisitions, and ensuring compliance with changing laws. An attorney's guidance in these scenarios can prevent costly mistakes and provide peace of mind, allowing you to focus on growing your business.

Selecting the right attorney, one who aligns with your LLC's needs, is fundamental. Start by identifying lawyers who specialize in business law or the specific areas most relevant to your business, such as intellectual property, employment, or real estate. Referrals from trusted colleagues or professional networks can be invaluable here. When meeting potential candidates, assess not only their expertise and experience but also their communication skills and understanding of your business vision. A good lawyer should be someone you feel comfortable discussing your business strategies with and who shows a commitment to helping you achieve your objectives.

Beyond handling immediate legal issues, retaining legal counsel for ongoing consultation can offer significant advantages. This proactive approach involves regular check-ins and updates with your lawyer to ensure that your business remains compliant with laws and regulations and is prepared for potential legal issues before they arise. Such an arrangement can help you navigate complexities like new employment laws, tax obligations, and industry-specific regulations that could impact your LLC. The ongoing relationship means your attorney becomes increasingly familiar with your business, providing tailored advice that can prevent legal issues and facilitate swift resolution when challenges arise.

Legal audits are another tool at your disposal. These are comprehensive examinations conducted by your attorney to review and assess all legal aspects of your business. This includes analyzing contracts, ensuring regulatory compliance, checking the adequacy of insurance coverage, and safeguarding intellectual property. Regular legal audits can identify potential legal vulnerabilities early, allowing you to address them proactively rather than reactively. This not only helps in avoiding litigation but also strengthens your business's foundation by ensuring all operations are up to legal standards.

The strategic integration of legal counsel into the management of your LLC transforms legal support from a mere expense to a vital investment in your business's stability and growth. By recognizing when to seek legal advice, choosing the right attorney, engaging in ongoing legal consultation, and utilizing legal audits, you enhance your ability to navigate the legal landscapes that influence your business.

As we close this chapter, remember that the role of legal counsel is not just about managing crises—it's about creating an environment where your business can grow securely and sustainably. In the next chapter, we will explore innovative strategies for maintaining and boosting your LLC's operational efficiency, ensuring that your business continues to evolve and succeed in an ever-changing economic landscape.

MAXIMIZING YOUR LLC'S POTENTIAL

$\mathcal{A}$s you navigate the ever-evolving business landscape, understanding and implementing advanced tax strategies can significantly enhance your LLC's financial health and operational efficiency. An effective tax planning allows you to steer your business towards greater profitability and stability. This chapter delves into innovative tax planning strategies specifically designed for LLCs, helping you uncover potential savings and benefits that can be reinvested into your business to fuel growth and innovation.

INNOVATIVE TAX PLANNING FOR LLCS

Election of S Corporation Taxation: Benefits and Considerations

Choosing the right tax status for your LLC can have profound implications on your financial landscape. One strategic option available for LLCs is electing to be taxed as an S Corporation. This election can be particularly advantageous for LLCs that have grown beyond their initial phase and are looking to optimize their tax obligations. By electing S Corporation status, you can potentially reduce self-employment taxes on some of your earnings, as profits and losses are passed through to shareholders who report them on their individual tax returns. However, not all LLC earnings are subject to employment tax; only the salary paid to the owner-employee is subject to payroll taxes, while remaining profits are subject to income tax only.

This structure is not without its considerations. The election involves strict eligibility criteria, including limits on the number and type of shareholders and adherence to specific guidelines regarding profit and loss allocation. Additionally, S Corporations are subject to closer scrutiny by tax authorities, particularly concerning reasonable salary payments to owner-employees. Therefore, it's crucial to weigh the potential tax benefits against the administrative responsibilities and compliance requirements. Consulting with a tax professional who understands the nuances of S Corporation status can provide useful insights and help you determine whether this election aligns with your business goals.

Advanced Deduction Strategies: Leveraging Less Commonly Known Deductions

Beyond the standard deductions commonly utilized by many businesses, there exist several lesser-known deductions that can yield significant tax savings for LLCs. These include deductions for charitable contributions, certain types of insurance premiums, and expenses related to business use of your home. For instance, if your LLC donates to qualified charities, these contributions may be deductible. Similarly, premiums for business interruption insurance, which can be crucial in maintaining financial stability during unforeseen disruptions, are often deductible as business expenses.

Moreover, if you use part of your home for business, you may qualify for a home office deduction, which considers expenses like utilities, property taxes, and repairs related to the portion of your home used for business. Maximizing these deductions requires a thorough understanding of tax laws and diligent record-keeping to substantiate the expenses. Implementing a robust accounting system and regularly consulting with tax advisors can help ensure that you are not only compliant with tax regulations but are also optimizing your tax benefits.

Tax Credits for LLCs: An Overview

Tax credits are a direct reduction of your tax liability, making them a highly valuable element of tax strategy for LLCs. Numerous federal and state tax credits are available, depending on your business activities and location. Examples include the Research and Development (R&D) Tax Credit, which rewards businesses that engage in qualifying research activities with a substantial tax credit. For LLCs involved in developing new products, processes, or software, this credit can offset the costs associated with innovative projects.

Additionally, small business health care tax credits are available for LLCs that provide health insurance to their employees. This credit is designed to make it more affordable for small businesses to offer health insurance benefits. Each tax credit has specific qualifications and rules, and the process of claiming these credits can be complex. Regularly exploring newly instituted tax credits and reassessing your eligibility can uncover new opportunities to reduce your tax burden and reinvest those savings back into your business.

Retirement Planning: Utilizing Retirement Plans as a Tax Strategy

Incorporating retirement planning into your tax strategy not only secures your financial future but can also provide immediate tax benefits. For LLC owners, setting up retirement plans such as a Simplified Employee Pension (SEP) IRA or a solo 401(k) can offer significant tax advantages. Contributions to these plans are typically tax-deductible, reducing your taxable income and thereby lowering your current tax liability. Additionally, these funds grow tax-deferred until withdrawal, providing a dual benefit of saving for retirement while optimizing current tax obligations.

The choice between different retirement plans depends on factors such as your income level, whether you have employees, and how much you can or want to contribute annually. For instance, a SEP IRA allows contributions of up to 25% of each employee's pay (including your own as the owner), while a solo 401(k) might be more suitable if you have no employees other than your spouse. Planning for retirement through these vehicles requires careful consideration of your long-term financial goals and current tax planning needs, making it advisable to work with financial advisors who specialize in retirement planning for business owners.

By embracing these innovative tax strategies, you position your LLC not just to survive but to thrive. Each decision you make regarding taxes can have ripple effects on your business's cash flow, growth potential, and long-term viability. As you continue to navigate the complexities of tax planning, remember that each strategy you implement is a step toward maximizing your business's potential and securing its future success.

BUILDING A BRAND AND COMMUNITY ENGAGEMENT

Crafting a unique brand identity is not merely about choosing a catchy name or an eye-catching logo; it involves a deep understanding of who your target audience is, what they need, and how your brand can uniquely meet those needs. When your brand identity resonates with your audience, it transforms first-time buyers into lifelong customers and turns casual browsers into brand advocates. Begin by defining your brand's mission, vision, and values—these should align closely with the expectations and aspirations of your target demographic.

Further solidify your brand identity through consistent messaging across all platforms. This consistency helps to build a reliable and recognizable brand that people feel they know and can trust. Every point of communication—be it your website, your packaging, or your customer service—should reinforce the same values and aesthetic. This coherence tells a compelling story that appeals to your audience's emotions and values, making your brand a part of their identity.

Content marketing is a powerful tool to build authority, engage with your community, and strengthen your brand. It involves creating and sharing content that is not directly promotional but is intended to stimulate interest in your products or services. For example, a blog post for a legal consultation LLC might provide insights into navigating small business licenses and permits—a topic that would engage and provide real value to prospective clients. Engaging content can establish your brand as a thought leader in your industry, building trust and credibility among your audience. Moreover, by optimizing this content for search engines, you can attract new traffic to your site, increasing your brand's visibility and reach.

Community building is another cornerstone of effective brand engagement. Creating a loyal community around your brand can be achieved through various strategies, including active social media engagement and event sponsorships. Social media platforms provide a direct way to interact with your audience, allowing for real-time communication and fostering a sense of community. Share behind-the-scenes content, respond to comments, and participate in relevant conversations to keep your audience engaged and invested in your brand. Additionally, sponsoring or participating in community events can increase your brand's visibility and strengthen community ties. These events provide an opportunity for potential customers to experience your brand firsthand, building familiarity and preference.

Corporate Social Responsibility (CSR) initiatives can significantly enhance your brand's reputation and foster community loyalty. By taking part in or initiating projects that contribute positively to society, your brand not only does good but also aligns its values with those of its customers, which can be particularly important if your target audience values ethical responsibility. For instance, an LLC that manufactures sports equipment might sponsor youth sports programs, supporting community health and wellness while also aligning with its customers' interests in sports and fitness. These CSR activities should be chosen based on their relevance to both your brand and your audience, ensuring that they reinforce your brand's values and resonate with your audience's expectations.

Incorporating these strategies into your brand development and community engagement efforts can transform your LLC from just another choice in the market to a preferred and trusted brand that stands out in the competitive landscape. By continuously nurturing these relationships and staying true to your brand's identity and values, you create a strong, loyal community that not only supports but also advocates for your business.

UTILIZING TECHNOLOGY FOR COMPETITIVE ADVANTAGE

In a marketplace where the pace of technological change is constantly accelerating, staying ahead of the latest tech trends is not just a strategic asset; it's a necessity for maintaining a competitive edge. As an entrepreneur, integrating cutting-edge technology into your business operations can significantly enhance efficiency and foster innovation. One of the most impactful trends is the adoption of cloud computing, which offers scalable infrastructure solutions that can grow with your business. This technology allows for the efficient handling of big data, providing you with actionable insights that can drive business decisions. Additionally, the integration of the *Internet of Things (IoT) devices* can streamline operations and improve data accuracy, from inventory management systems that automatically update stock levels to sensors that monitor equipment performance to prevent downtime.

Another area where technology is making a substantial impact is through *Artificial Intelligence (AI)* and machine learning, which can be applied in various aspects of business operations to optimize both efficiency and customer interactions. For example, AI-driven analytics can predict customer behavior, enabling personalized marketing strategies that significantly increase conversion rates. Moreover, machine learning algorithms can optimize logistics and supply chain management, predicting and mitigating potential disruptions and thereby enhancing operational reliability.

E-commerce strategies have evolved significantly with advancements in technology, particularly through the customization and personalization of the shopping experience. Utilizing AI to analyze customer data collected from various touchpoints allows businesses to offer personalized recommendations, tailored email marketing, and targeted promotions that speak directly to the individual consumer's preferences and previous behavior. This level of personalization not only enhances the customer experience but also boosts loyalty and sales. For instance, an online retailer could use AI to suggest products that complement a previous purchase, increasing the likelihood of a repeat sale.

Mobile Optimization: Enhancing Reach and Engagement

With the increasing prevalence of smartphones, ensuring that your digital presence is optimized for mobile users is crucial. Mobile optimization involves designing your website and e-commerce platforms to offer a seamless user experience on mobile devices, ensuring fast load times, easy navigation, and accessible information. This is vital as mobile commerce continues to grow, with more consumers than ever making purchases directly from their smartphones. A mobile-optimized site not only improves user engagement but also boosts search engine rankings, as search engines favor websites that provide a good mobile experience.

The importance of mobile optimization extends to all facets of your digital presence, including email marketing and social media. Emails should be formatted to display correctly on mobile devices, with clear calls to action that are easy to click on a smaller screen. Similarly, social media content should be created with mobile users in mind, considering how images, videos, and text will appear on various devices. By ensuring that every digital touchpoint is optimized for mobile, you enhance your accessibility and appeal to a broader audience, which is increasingly likely to interact with your brand on-the-go.

Tech-Driven Customer Service Solutions: Improving Satisfaction and Efficiency

In today's digital age, customer expectations for quick and efficient service are higher than ever. Implementing technology solutions such as chatbots and AI can significantly enhance your customer service capabilities. Chatbots can handle a large volume of simple customer queries without human intervention, providing instant responses around the clock. This not only improves customer satisfaction by offering immediate assistance but also frees up your customer service team to handle more complex issues, thereby increasing overall efficiency.

Moreover, AI can be used to analyze customer service interactions and identify areas for improvement, such as common complaints or questions that could be addressed more effectively. This ongoing analysis helps in refining your customer service strategies, ensuring that they continue to meet customer needs and enhance satisfaction. Additionally, AI-driven tools can personalize customer service interactions by accessing individual customer data, providing service representatives with a comprehensive view of the customer's history and preferences, which enables more personalized and effective support.

By leveraging these technological advancements, your LLC can not only improve operational efficiencies and customer engagement but also stay ahead of the curve in a rapidly evolving business environment. Technology, when strategically integrated into business practices, not only drives growth but also solidifies your position as an innovative leader in your industry.

SUSTAINABLE PRACTICES FOR LONG-TERM LLC SUCCESS

Economic Sustainability: Strategies for Ensuring the Longevity of Your LLC

Economic sustainability involves more than just surviving the fiscal year; it's about setting up your LLC for long-term financial health. This requires a keen understanding of your business model, market conditions, and the economic environment. *Diversification* is a key strategy in this regard. By expanding your product lines or entering new markets, you can reduce dependence on a single source of revenue, which can be crucial in times of market uncertainty. For example, if your primary product is seasonal, developing complementary products or services that have different peak times can help maintain steady revenue throughout the year.

Another essential aspect of economic sustainability is rigorous financial planning. Regular financial reviews can help you stay on top of your cash flow, identify potential financial challenges before they arise, and adjust your strategies accordingly. Tools like *financial forecasting models* can also be helpful, providing insights into how future scenarios might affect your business. Engaging with financial advisors to review and refine your investment strategies can further enhance your economic resilience, ensuring that your assets are working as hard as they can for your business.

Social Sustainability: Engaging in Responsible Practices

Social sustainability focuses on the impact your business has on society, including how you treat your employees, how you engage with your community, and the integrity with which you conduct your business. Fair labor practices are not only a legal requirement but are also crucial for maintaining a motivated and productive workforce. Practices such as offering fair wages, ensuring safe working conditions, and providing opportunities for employee development can help foster a loyal and engaged team. Furthermore, involving your business in community initiatives can strengthen your local ties and enhance your brand's reputation. Whether it's sponsoring a local event, participating in community service, or supporting a local charity, these activities can greatly enhance your social footprint.

Your business's commitment to ethical practices should also extend to your supply chain. Conducting regular audits of your suppliers to ensure they adhere to ethical standards regarding labor and environmental practices is critical. This not only helps prevent potential scandals that could harm your brand but also supports the broader goal of global sustainability. Transparent communication about these efforts, through sustainability reports or updates on your website, can help build trust with your customers and stakeholders, showing that your commitment to social responsibility is comprehensive and genuine.

Sustainability Reporting: Enhancing Transparency and Trust

Sustainability reporting is a powerful tool that can help communicate your commitment to sustainable practices to your stakeholders and the broader public. These reports provide detailed insights into your environmental, economic, and social initiatives and their outcomes. Developing a comprehensive sustainability report involves collecting data on key performance indicators related to sustainability, such as energy usage, waste management, employee turnover rates, and community engagement activities. This data should be presented in a clear and accessible format, often supported by case studies or testimonials that illustrate your achievements.

Moreover, sustainability reporting is not just about showcasing current successes; it's also about setting goals for the future. This forward-looking approach demonstrates a proactive stance on sustainability, showing that your LLC is committed to continuous improvement. Engaging stakeholders in this process can also provide important feedback that can help shape future initiatives. Regularly updating your sustainability reports, ideally on an annual basis, ensures that your stakeholders are kept informed of your progress and can see the tangible impacts of their support.

By integrating these sustainable practices into the core operations of your LLC, you not only enhance your immediate business environment but also contribute to the broader global efforts towards sustainability. These practices help build a resilient business that can adapt to changes, meet the challenges of the modern world, and continue to thrive in the long term. As you move forward, consider each of these aspects of sustainability as integral components of your business strategy, essential for ensuring the continued success and relevance of your LLC in an increasingly conscientized market.

INTERNATIONAL EXPANSION: TAKING YOUR LLC GLOBAL

Venturing into new global markets can significantly enhance your brand's reach and profitability but comes with its set of complexities and challenges. Key to this transition is conducting robust market research. This critical first step involves delving deep into understanding which countries offer a fertile ground for your products or services. This process should be meticulous and data-driven, involving analysis of market size, consumer behavior, competition, and market entry barriers. Tools such as global market databases and insights from international trade bodies can provide critical data, while primary research methods, like surveys and focus groups, offer nuanced insights into local consumer preferences and needs.

Equally important is understanding the competitive landscape. Identifying who your competitors will be, their market share, and their business models can provide insights into potential challenges and opportunities for differentiation. Additionally, assessing the economic and political stability of potential markets is crucial, as these factors can significantly impact business operations.

Navigating the complex legal and regulatory landscape of international business is another critical area that requires careful planning and strategy. Each country has its own set of laws and regulations that can impact various aspects of your business operations, from product standards and labor laws to import restrictions and tax regulations. Ensuring compliance with these laws is not only crucial for lawful operations but also for maintaining your business's reputation. Understanding the nuances of international trade agreements and treaties can aid in making informed decisions about market entry strategies.

Cultural adaptation is crucial when expanding internationally. What works in your home market may not resonate with consumers in a new country. Adapting your business practices, product offerings, and marketing strategies to align with local cultures, tastes, and preferences is essential for success. This might involve modifying product designs, changing marketing messages, or even adjusting business models to better suit local practices and consumer behaviors. Moreover, cultural sensitivity and awareness can help in building trust and relationships with local stakeholders, which are crucial for business success in foreign markets.

Finally, managing logistics and supply chain in international markets is a significant challenge but critical to ensuring efficient operations. Factors such as transportation costs, lead times, local infrastructure, and reliability of local suppliers must be considered. Developing a robust logistics strategy that includes diversifying suppliers and considering local manufacturing options can mitigate risks associated with supply chain disruptions. Advanced planning for logistics can also help in managing costs and ensuring timely delivery of products, which is crucial for customer satisfaction and retention in new markets.

By carefully planning and implementing strategies across these areas, your LLC can effectively manage the complexities of international expansion and tap into new growth opportunities.

SUCCESS STORIES: LESSONS FROM SUCCESSFUL LLCS

By examining a variety of successful Limited Liability Companies (LLCs), we can extract observations and strategies that are applicable across different industries. These case studies not only spotlight the paths these businesses have navigated but also underscore the importance of adaptability and innovation in their success. Let's delve into several examples to understand how these companies have not only flourished but also how they managed to turn challenges into stepping stones for growth.

One illustrative case is that of a tech startup that began as a small LLC and grew to become a major player in the software as a service (SaaS) industry. Initially, the company faced intense competition and struggled to secure a foothold in the market. However, through a strategic pivot from a service-based model to a product-based approach, they were able to differentiate themselves. This pivot was not simple; it required a complete overhaul of their operational structure and product delivery model. The key lesson here is the value of flexibility in business strategy and the importance of being willing to reassess and adjust the business model in response to market feedback and changing conditions.

Another example comes from a green energy company that utilized state and federal tax credits to scale their operations rapidly. This LLC strategically navigated the complexities of the renewable energy credits system to fund their expansion, demonstrating the importance of a deep understanding of relevant regulations and available incentives. This approach not only provided them with the necessary capital to grow but also aligned perfectly with their commitment to sustainable business practices, enhancing their brand reputation and consumer trust.

These stories underline the significance of innovation—whether in transforming business models or in leveraging regulatory frameworks to support growth. Innovation serves as a catalyst for differentiation and can be a decisive factor in gaining a competitive edge. These companies didn't just adapt to changes; they anticipated or created changes that propelled their businesses forward.

Furthermore, overcoming obstacles is a common theme across successful LLCs. For instance, a boutique fashion retailer expanded from an online-only presence to multiple physical locations by overcoming significant logistical challenges. The transition involved not just a scaling of operations but a recalibration of their supply chain to meet the demands of physical inventory management and customer service excellence. Their strategy included rigorous market research to select store locations and a phased rollout plan to manage the financial risks associated with expansion. This example shows that meticulous planning and strategic risk management are crucial in overcoming operational challenges and achieving sustainable growth.

These narratives not only inspire but also instruct. They highlight that the path to success is not linear but requires continuous learning, agility, and the readiness to innovate. By understanding these stories, other LLCs can glean insights into not just surviving but thriving in the business world.

As we wrap up this exploration of successful LLCs, remember that the core lessons revolve around the flexibility to pivot, the acumen to harness regulatory and financial frameworks, and the innovation to differentiate.

BONUS CHAPTER

LLC STARTER CHECKLIST

*C*reating an LLC, or Limited Liability Company, is a popular choice for many entrepreneurs because it offers legal protection by separating personal and business liabilities. Here's a detailed LLC starter checklist that will guide anyone through the key steps to establishing an LLC successfully:

Step 1. Choose a Business Name

- **Check Availability:** Ensure the name is not already in use by another company in your state by checking with your state's business entity registry. https://dos.fl.gov/sunbiz/search/

- **Follow Naming Rules:** Your state may have specific

naming requirements, such as including "LLC" in the name.

- **Consider Trademark:** Check if the name is available for trademark or has existing trademarks that could conflict. https://search.sunbiz.org/Inquiry/CorporationSearch/ByTrademark

Step 2. Select a Registered Agent

- **Role of Registered Agent:** This is an individual or service authorized to receive legal and tax documents on behalf of your LLC.

- **Requirements:** Must be a resident of the state where the LLC is registered, or a company authorized to do business in that state.

- **Search term**: Search Google for the term: "llc register agents" and you will get a list of registered agents in your state.

Step 3. File Articles of Organization

- **Document Preparation:** Prepare the necessary paperwork, typically called the Articles of Organization, which includes details like your LLC name, address, and the registered agent's name and address.

- **Filing With State:** Submit your Articles of Organization to the state's business filing agency along with the required filing fee. Typically, the Secretary of State will be the filing agency.

Step 4. Create an Operating Agreement

- **Purpose:** Although not required in all states, an operating agreement is crucial for outlining the ownership and operating procedures of your LLC. Search Google for the term: "samples of LLC Operating Agreements" for a list of Registered Agents in your state.

- **Contents:** Include information about member duties, investment percentages, dispute resolution, and what happens if a member leaves the business.

Step 5. Obtain an EIN (Employer Identification Number)

- **Application:** Apply for an EIN via the IRS website or by mail. This number is essentially a social security number for your business and is necessary for tax purposes. https://www.irs.gov/businesses/small-businesses-self-employed/apply-for-an-employer-identification-number-ein-online

- **Cost:** There is no cost to apply for an EIN.

Step 6. Register for State and Local Taxes

- **Requirements:** Depending on your business type, location, and whether you have employees, you may need to register for various state and local taxes.

- **Common Taxes:** These can include sales tax, payroll tax, and any other industry-specific taxes.

Step 7. Comply with Licensing and Permit Requirements

- **Research:** Determine what specific permits and licenses are required for your business type at both the state and local level.

- **Apply:** Obtain all necessary licenses and permits before starting business operations.

Step 8. Announce Your Business

- **Publication Requirement:** Some states require that new LLCs publish a notice in a local newspaper. This typically includes the LLC's formation and other legal information.

Step 9. Set Up a Business Bank Account

- **Purpose:** Keep your business finances separate from personal accounts to maintain the liability protection that an LLC provides.

- **Requirements:** Typically, you need your EIN, a copy of the Articles of Organization, and a resolution identifying authorized signers if more than one person is involved in the LLC.

Step 10. Review Compliance and Reporting Requirements

- **Annual Reports:** Most states require LLCs to file an annual report and possibly pay a yearly fee.

- **Ongoing Compliance:** Stay updated on changes in laws that could affect your LLC's operations and compliance.

Step 11. Consider Business Insurance

- **Types of Insurance:** Depending on your business, consider liability insurance, property insurance, professional liability, or workers' compensation.

- **Protection:** Insurance can protect your business from various risks and liabilities beyond the legal structure of an LLC.

By following these steps, you can ensure that your LLC is set up correctly and compliantly, offering a solid foundation for your business endeavors. Regularly review each step to adapt to changes in your business environment and regulatory updates.

NOTE: Always check with your specific State's guidelines and laws before registering your LLC.

LLC TIME MANAGEMENT PLAN

Creating a comprehensive LLC Business Time Management Plan involves structuring a strategy that can adapt to the dynamic needs of your company while improving productivity and efficiency. Below, I'll outline a step-by-step plan tailored for an LLC, focusing on effective allocation and optimization of time resources.

LLC Business Time Management Plan

Step 1. Assessment of Current Time Management Practices

- **Objective:** To identify strengths, weaknesses, and opportunities in current workflows and time management practices.

- **Action Steps:**

1. Conduct a time audit across different departments to understand how time is currently being spent.
2. Survey team members to gather insights on perceived bottlenecks and inefficiencies.
3. Analyze project completion rates and deadlines to identify patterns of delays or early completions.

Step 2. Goal Setting and Prioritization

- **Objective:** To align time management strategies with business objectives and prioritize tasks that add the most value.

- **Action Steps:**

1. Define clear, measurable short-term and long-term goals for the business.
2. Use tools like the Eisenhower Box to help categorize tasks by urgency and importance. See sample using Asana app: https://asana.com/templates/eisenhower-matrix

3. Develop a prioritization matrix for projects based on their potential impact and resource requirements.

Step 3. Time Allocation Strategy

- **Objective:** To create a structured approach for allocating time to tasks and projects effectively.

- **Action Steps:**

1. Implement time blocking techniques to dedicate specific hours to focused work without interruptions.
2. Use project management software to set up a visual representation of timelines and deadlines. Check out this project management tool for up to 10 users: https://nulab.com/backlog-lp/project-management/
3. Allocate buffer times between tasks to account for overruns and unexpected complications.

Step 4. Optimization of Processes and Workflows

- **Objective:** To streamline operations and reduce time wastage.

- **Action Steps:**

1. Identify repetitive tasks and explore automation options.
2. Review and optimize workflow processes every quarter to ensure they are the most efficient.
3. Encourage cross-departmental communication to enhance coordination and reduce duplicated efforts.

Step 5. Leadership and Employee Engagement

- **Objective:** To foster a culture that values time management and personal accountability.

- **Action Steps:**

1. Train leaders on time management techniques and tools they can share with their teams.
2. Regularly communicate the importance of time management through workshops and team meetings.
3. Set up a reward system for teams and individuals who achieve their goals efficiently.

Step 6. Technology Integration

- **Objective:** To leverage technology to enhance time management practices.

- **Action Steps:**

1. Evaluate and implement task management and collaboration tools that fit the company's operational needs.
2. Use data analytics to track time management improvements and make informed decisions.
3. Ensure all team members are trained on any new technologies introduced.

Step 7. Monitoring, Review, and Continuous Improvement

- **Objective:** To continuously assess the effectiveness of time management strategies and make necessary adjustments.

- **Action Steps:**

1. Establish key performance indicators (KPIs) related to time management and review them regularly.
2. Schedule monthly review meetings to discuss progress and tackle any challenges.
3. Encourage feedback from employees on time management practices and use it to refine strategies.

Step 8. Adaptation to Market Dynamics

- **Objective:** To ensure the business can quickly adapt to changes without significant time losses.

- **Action Steps:**

1. Keep abreast of industry trends and technological advancements that can influence time management.
2. Regularly reassess external factors such as market conditions and competitor activities to adjust time management plans accordingly.

Conclusion

This LLC Business Time Management Plan serves as a roadmap to help your company streamline operations, enhance productivity, and maintain a competitive edge. By adhering to this plan and regularly updating it in response to internal feedback and external changes, your LLC can not only manage time effectively but also adapt quickly to new challenges and opportunities.

PRODUCTIVITY IDEAS FOR YOUR LLC BUSINESS

Running an LLC efficiently involves juggling various tasks and responsibilities. Here's a comprehensive list of productivity ideas specifically tailored for LLC businesses that can help streamline operations, enhance team collaboration, and ultimately drive growth.

Leverage Technology

- **Automated Accounting Software:** Utilize tools like *QuickBooks*, *FreshBooks*, or *Xero* for managing finances, tracking expenses, and invoicing.
- **Project Management Tools:** Adopt platforms like *Asana*, *Trello*, or *Monday.com* to keep projects on track and enhance team collaboration.
- **Customer Relationship Management (CRM):** Implement a CRM system like *Salesforce* or *HubSpot* to manage customer interactions and data throughout the customer lifecycle.

Streamline Communication

- **Centralized Communication Platforms:** Use *Slack*, *Microsoft Teams*, or *Google Chat* to reduce email overload and ensure faster, more efficient team communication.
- **Regular Check-Ins:** Schedule regular meetings (daily or weekly) to update on progress, address issues, and align team goals.

Implement Effective Time Management

- **Time Tracking Tools:** Encourage the use of tools like *Toggl* or *Harvest* to help team members keep track of how much time they spend on various tasks.
- **Priority Setting:** Adopt the *Eisenhower Box* technique to help prioritize tasks based on urgency and importance. Sample: https://asana.com/templates/eisenhower-matrix

Optimize Legal and Administrative Processes

- **Online Legal Services:** Use platforms like *LegalZoom* or *Rocket Lawyer* for routine legal tasks such as contract reviews or trademark filings.
- **Virtual Assistants:** Hire virtual assistance for handling administrative tasks like scheduling, email management, or customer support.

Focus on Employee Training and Development

- **Regular Training:** Invest in continuous learning opportunities for staff through online courses, webinars, or workshops.
- **Cross-Training:** Encourage employees to learn different aspects of the business to improve versatility and coverage during absences.

Adopt Lean Practices

- **Regular Audits:** Conduct regular audits of business processes to identify inefficiencies or redundant tasks.

- **Continuous Improvement:** Foster a culture of continuous improvement by encouraging feedback and suggestions from all team members.

Enhance Online Presence

- **SEO Optimization:** Regularly update your website and use SEO best practices to attract more organic traffic.
- **Social Media Automation:** Use tools like *Buffer* or *Hootsuite* to schedule posts and manage social media platforms efficiently.

Develop a Flexible Work Environment

- **Remote Work Options:** Offer flexible working conditions where possible to increase employee satisfaction and productivity.
- **Flexible Hours:** Allow flexible working hours as long as the work gets done and meetings are attended.

Financial Management

- **Budgeting Tools:** Use apps like *Mint* or *YNAB* (You Need A Budget) to keep track of business finances and plan budgets effectively.
- **Financial Forecasting:** Regularly forecast financials to predict and prepare for future financial needs and challenges.

Regular Networking and Collaboration

- **Industry Events:** Attend or host webinars and workshops to stay connected with industry trends and network with peers.
- **Partnerships:** Look for partnership opportunities with other businesses that can offer complementary services to your clients.

Implementing these productivity strategies can help streamline operations, improve efficiency, and foster a proactive work environment in your LLC. It's all about finding the right balance between technology, people, and processes to drive your business forward.

CONCLUSION

As we reach the end of this exciting journey through the intricacies of forming and managing a Limited Liability Company, it's essential to pause and reflect on the ground we've covered. From the initial chapters where we laid down the basics of LLCs, exploring their benefits and legal structures, to advanced management strategies, taxation nuances, and essential growth tactics, this guide has aimed to equip you with the knowledge needed to establish a robust foundation for your business.

We've traversed through the critical importance of selecting the right business structure, emphasized the protective shield an LLC offers to your personal assets, decoded the complex landscape of taxation, and unveiled strategies that bolster growth and ensure sustainability. Each section was crafted with the goal of empowering you as an entrepreneur or small business owner, enhancing your ability to navigate the business world with confidence and acumen.

You now possess the insights and tools necessary to confidently form, manage, and maintain your LLC, laying down a strong and resilient foundation for your business venture.

I encourage you to step forward into your entrepreneurial journey with renewed vigor. Whether it's drafting or revising your business plan, consulting with a legal or financial advisor, or taking a small but significant step toward establishing your LLC, the time to act is now. Use the strategies, knowledge, and tools you've acquired to carve out a successful path for your business.

I also urge you to continue your education, subscribe to relevant publications, join business associations, and participate in workshops or seminars to keep your knowledge fresh and applicable.

Starting and running a business comes with its challenges, but with the right information and resources, you are well-equipped to overcome them. Remember, you are not alone in this journey. The entrepreneurial path is trodden by many who share your aspirations and challenges. Draw strength from this community and always reach out for support when needed.

Thank you for investing your time and energy in reading this book. It has been a privilege to share this knowledge with you, and I hope it serves as a valuable tool in your arsenal as you build and grow your business. May your entrepreneurial journey be prosperous, informed, and fulfilling.

LEAVE A 1-CLICK REVIEW

Customer Reviews

☆☆☆☆☆ 2
5.0 out of 5 stars ▾

5 star		100%
4 star		0%
3 star		0%
2 star		0%
1 star		0%

See all verified purchase reviews ›

Share your thoughts with other customers

Write a customer review ⬅

I would be incredibly thankful if you take just
60-seconds to write a brief review on Amazon,
even if it's just a few sentences!

https://amazon.com/review/create-review?asin=1960188305

ABOUT THE AUTHOR

Conrad Presley has an academic background in psychology and sociology that uniquely positions him to explore and explain the deep-rooted psychological and social factors that underpin enduring conflicts.

Presley's journey began with his fervent curiosity about human behavior and societal dynamics. This intellectual pursuit led him to get advanced degrees in both fields, equipping him with a nuanced perspective on the intricate interplay between individual psychology and societal structures.

As owner of several successful businesses, he enjoys mentoring entrepreneurs and believes that by helping others succeed, we can all make the world a better place.

In sum, Conrad is a bridge-builder, connecting psychology, sociology, and his business experience to offer insightful and impactful strategies for personal growth and professional success. His unique perspective on human behavior and societal dynamics has made him a highly sought-after consultant in various industries. By drawing from his vast knowledge and real-world experience, Conrad continues to inspire individuals and organizations to reach their full potential.

BIBLIOGRAPHY

LLC Annual Fees by State - All 50 States (2024 Costs) https://www.llcuniversity.com/llc-annual-fees-by-state/

LLC vs. Corporation: How Are They Different? (2024) - Shopify https://www.shopify.com/blog/llc-vs-corporation

Articles of Organization: Definition, What's Included, and ... https://www.investopedia.com/terms/a/articles-of-organization.asp

How to choose an LLC name: Tips for naming your LLC https://www.legalzoom.com/articles/how-to-choose-an-llc-name

5 Factors to Consider When Choosing a Registered Agent https://www.harborcompliance.com/blog/5-factors-to-consider-when-choosing-a-registered-agent/

10 Must Haves in an LLC Operating Agreement https://gouchevlaw.com/top-10-must-haves-llc-operating-agreement/

LLC Tax Benefits Guide for Small Businesses - MarketWatch https://www.marketwatch.com/guides/business/llc-tax-benefits/#:~:text=The%20Tax%20Cuts%20and%20Jobs,income%20taxes%20with%20this%20deduction

Best Small Business Accounting Software of 2023 https://www.usnews.com/360-reviews/business/best-small-business-accounting-software

LLC Tax and Reporting Requirements https://www.wolterskluwer.com/en/expert-insights/llc-tax-and-reporting-requirements

LLC Record-Keeping: Best Practices for Organizing and ... https://www.linkedin.com/pulse/llc-record-keeping-best-practices-organizing-managing-hearn-ed-d

Best Accounting Software for Small Businesses of May 2024 https://www.nerdwallet.com/best/small-business/accounting-software

Startup Cash Flow Management: Unlocking The Secrets https://www.zeni.ai/blog/startup-cash-flow-management

50 Small Business Marketing Ideas for 2024 https://blog.hubspot.com/marketing/small-business-marketing-guide

Can you hire employees in an LLC? - LegalZoom https://www.legalzoom.com/articles/can-you-hire-employees-in-an-llc

State Guide to LLC Report and Tax Filing Requirements https://www.nolo.com/legal-encyclopedia/50-state-guide-annual-report-tax-filing-requirements-llcs

What Every Small Business Should Know About ... https://www.uschamber.com/co/start/strategy/intellectual-property-what-small-businesses-should-know

LLC Insurance: Best Options for Your Business in 2023 https://www.nerdwallet.com/article/small-business/llc-business-insurance

Succession Planning for an LLC: Ensuring a Smooth ... https://www.linkedin.com/pulse/succession-planning-llc-ensuring-smooth-transition-future-9cnuc?trk=public_post_main-feed-card_feed-article-content

9 Small Business Growth Strategies for 2023 | CO https://www.uschamber.com/co/start/strategy/best-small-business-growth-strategies

Fund your business | U.S. Small Business Administration https://www.sba.gov/business-guide/plan-your-business/fund-your-business

Strategies That Fit Emerging Markets https://hbr.org/2005/06/strategies-that-fit-emerging-markets

Scaling Automation: Two Proven Paths to Success https://sloanreview.mit.edu/article/scaling-automation-two-proven-paths-to-success

How to Protect Your Assets Using an LLC https://www.newburnlaw.com/how-to-protect-your-assets-using-an-llc

U.S. State Privacy Laws in 2023: California, Colorado, Connecticut, Utah, and Virginia https://www.lockelord.com/newsandevents/publications/2022/12/us-state-privacy-laws-2023

Chapter 7 Bankruptcy for LLCs: Everything You Need To ... https://www.findlaw.com/bankruptcy/chapter-7/chapter-7-bankruptcy-for-llcs--everything-you-need-to-know.html

What are the Three Basic Types of Dispute Resolution? ... https://www.pon.harvard.edu/daily/dispute-resolution/what-are-the-three-basic-types-of-dispute-resolution-what-to-know-about-mediation-arbitration-and-litigation/

10 Small Business Tech Trends Defining 2023 https://builtin.com/articles/small-business-tech-trends

How To Build a Brand in 7 Steps: Get Started in 2024 https://www.shopify.com/blog/how-to-build-a-brand

7 well-known LLC examples from popular companies https://www.doola.com/blog/llc-examples/

Made in the USA
Coppell, TX
21 February 2025

46236292R10098